First World War
and Army of Occupation
War Diary
France, Belgium and Germany

29 DIVISION
86 Infantry Brigade
1 Battalion Royal Guernsey Light Infantry
26 September 1917 - 30 April 1918

WO95/2302/1

The Naval & Military Press Ltd
www.nmarchive.com
Published in association with The National Archives

Published by

The Naval & Military Press Ltd

Unit 10 Ridgewood Industrial Park,

Uckfield, East Sussex,

TN22 5QE England

Tel: +44 (0) 1825 749494

www.naval-military-press.com

www.nmarchive.com

This diary has been reprinted in facsimile from the original. Any imperfections are inevitably reproduced and the quality may fall short of modern type and cartographic standards.

© **Crown Copyright**
Images reproduced by permission of The National Archives, London, England, 2015.

Contents

Document type	Place/Title	Date From	Date To
Heading	WO95/2302/1		
Heading	29th Division 86th Infy Bde 1st Bn Roy. Guernsey Lt Infy Sept 1917-Apr 1918. To G.H.Q. Troop.		
Miscellaneous	D.A.G., 3rd Echelon, Base.	31/10/1917	31/10/1917
War Diary	Bourne Park Camp Canterbury	26/09/1917	26/09/1917
War Diary	Southampton.	26/09/1917	26/09/1917
War Diary	Havre.	27/09/1917	30/09/1917
War Diary	Proven.	01/10/1917	01/10/1917
Miscellaneous			
Operation(al) Order(s)	1st (S) Bn. Royal Guernsey Light Infantry. Operation Order (No. 1).	25/09/1917	25/09/1917
Operation(al) Order(s)	1st. Bn: Royal Guernsey L.I. Operation Order No. 2		
Operation(al) Order(s)	1st (S) Bn. Royal Guernsey L.I. Operation Order No. 3		
Operation(al) Order(s)	1st (S) Bn. R. Guernsey L.I. Operation Order No. 4	00/10/1917	00/10/1917
Miscellaneous	1st (S) Bn. Royal Guernsey Light Infantry. Operation Order (No. 1).	26/09/1917	26/09/1917
Operation(al) Order(s)	1st. Bn: Royal Guernsey L.I. Operation Order No. 3	25/09/1917	25/09/1917
Operation(al) Order(s)	1st. (S) Bn: Royal Guernsey L.I. Operation Order No. 3		
War Diary	Stoke Camp (F 5.d1.6).	02/10/1917	08/10/1917
War Diary	Parroy II Camp (B16 C 9.5).		
War Diary	Stoke Camp (F 5 d1.6).	15/10/1917	17/10/1917
War Diary	Peselhoek (A.26.b).	17/10/1917	17/10/1917
War Diary	Beaumitz (Q24.c.2).	18/10/1917	18/10/1917
War Diary	Hendecourt (X 17 a 4.6).	18/10/1917	31/10/1917
War Diary	Hendecourt (X 17.a.4.6).	30/10/1917	30/10/1917
Operation(al) Order(s)	1st (S) Bn. R. Guernsey. L.I. Operation Order No. 4	16/10/1917	16/10/1917
Miscellaneous	1st (S) Bn. R. Guernsey. L.I. Casualty List No. 1	31/10/1917	31/10/1917
Heading	War Diary R G LI Vol I		
War Diary	Bourne Park Camp Canterbury	26/09/1917	26/09/1917
War Diary	Southampton.	26/09/1917	26/09/1917
War Diary	Havre	27/09/1917	30/09/1917
War Diary	Proven.	01/10/1917	01/10/1917
War Diary	Stoke Camp (F 5 d.1.6).	02/10/1917	08/10/1917
War Diary	Parroy II Camp (B16.C.9.5).		
War Diary	Stoke Camp (F.5.d.1.6).	15/10/1917	17/10/1917
War Diary	Peselhoek (A.26.b).	17/10/1917	17/10/1917
War Diary	Beaumitz (Q 24 C 2).	18/10/1917	18/10/1917
War Diary	Hendecourt (X 17.a.4.6).	18/10/1917	31/10/1917
War Diary	Hendecourt (X.17.c.4.6).	30/10/1917	30/10/1917
Miscellaneous	D.A.G. 3rd Echelon.	20/12/1917	20/12/1917
War Diary	Hindicourt.	02/11/1917	17/11/1917
War Diary	Hautes Allaines.	18/11/1917	18/11/1917
War Diary		20/11/1917	20/11/1917
War Diary	Mine Wood.	21/11/1917	21/11/1917
War Diary	Marcoing.	23/11/1917	30/11/1917
Operation(al) Order(s)	1st (S) Batt. Royal Guernsey L.I. (Operation) Order No. 6	17/11/1917	17/11/1917
Miscellaneous	Must Be Completed By 7 a.m.		
Miscellaneous	Time Of Departure Of Train		
Operation(al) Order(s)	1st Bn. Royal Guernsey L.I. (Operation) Order No. 8	19/11/1917	19/11/1917

Miscellaneous	D.A.G. 3rd Echelon.	31/12/1917	31/12/1917
War Diary	Masniers	01/12/1917	02/12/1917
War Diary	Brown Line.	02/12/1917	02/12/1917
War Diary	Ribecourt	03/12/1917	03/12/1917
War Diary	Havrincourt Wood	04/12/1917	04/12/1917
War Diary	Fins.	05/12/1917	05/12/1917
War Diary	Houvin-Houvigneul	06/12/1917	16/12/1917
War Diary	Flers.	17/12/1917	17/12/1917
War Diary	Le Parcq	18/12/1917	18/12/1917
War Diary	Verchocq	19/12/1917	31/12/1917
Operation(al) Order(s)	1st (S) Bn. R. Guernsey. L.I. Move Order No. 1	15/12/1917	15/12/1917
Operation(al) Order(s)	1st (S) Bn. R. Guernsey. L.I. Move Order No. 2	16/12/1917	16/12/1917
Operation(al) Order(s)	1st (S) Bn. R. Guernsey. L.I. Move Order No. 3		
Miscellaneous	Sheet No. 2		
Miscellaneous	1st Bn. R. Guernsey L.I. Casualty List No. 3		
Miscellaneous	Sheet No. 3		
Miscellaneous	1st Bn: Royal Guernsey L.I. Casualty Report No. 5		
Miscellaneous	1st (S) Bn. R.G.S.I. Casualty List No. 2		
War Diary	Verchocq.	01/01/1918	03/01/1918
War Diary	Audenthun.	04/01/1918	14/01/1918
War Diary	Brandhoek.	16/01/1918	17/01/1918
War Diary	St. Jean.	18/01/1918	18/01/1918
War Diary	In The Line.	19/01/1918	26/01/1918
War Diary	Brake Camp.	28/01/1918	31/01/1918
Operation(al) Order(s)	1st Bn. R. Guernsey L.I. Operation Order No. 1		
Operation(al) Order(s)	1st Bn: R. Guernsey L.I. Move Order No. 4	02/01/1918	02/01/1918
Operation(al) Order(s)	1st Bn: R. Guernsey L.I. Move Order No. 5	13/01/1918	13/01/1918
Miscellaneous	1st R. Guernsey L.I. Relief Order.		
Miscellaneous	Rations for the 16th will be carried on the man.		
Miscellaneous		25/01/1918	25/01/1918
Heading	Rear H.Q.		
Miscellaneous	D.A.G., Base.	01/03/1918	01/03/1918
War Diary	Brake Camp.	01/02/1918	09/02/1918
War Diary	Hasler Camp	11/02/1918	12/02/1918
War Diary	Poperinghe.	12/02/1918	19/02/1918
War Diary	Eecke Area.	19/02/1918	28/02/1918
Miscellaneous	1st Division Royal Guernsey L.I. Relief Orders.	02/02/1918	02/02/1918
Miscellaneous	Move Order. 1st R. Guernsey Light Infantry.	10/02/1918	10/02/1918
Operation(al) Order(s)	1st Bn. Royal Guernsey L.I. Move Orders No. 6	18/02/1918	18/02/1918
War Diary	Eecke Area.	01/03/1918	07/03/1918
War Diary	Brandhoek Area	08/03/1918	08/03/1918
War Diary	Irish Farm Camp.	17/03/1918	17/03/1918
War Diary	Bellevue.	23/03/1918	23/03/1918
War Diary	California Camp.	27/03/1918	27/03/1918
War Diary	Bellevue.	29/03/1918	29/03/1918
Miscellaneous	1st Bn. R. Guernsey L.I. Casualty List No. 4		
Operation(al) Order(s)	Move Orders No. 8. 1st Bn: Royal Guernsey L.I.	07/03/1918	07/03/1918
Miscellaneous	Relief Order.	16/03/1918	16/03/1918
Miscellaneous	Distribution.		
Miscellaneous	Relief Order. 1st R.G.L.I.	23/03/1918	23/03/1918
Miscellaneous	Relief Order. 1. R.G.L.I.	26/03/1918	26/03/1918
Miscellaneous	Relief Order. 1/ R.G.L.I.	29/03/1918	29/03/1918
Miscellaneous	Casualty List No. 6	01/04/1918	01/04/1918
Operation(al) Order(s)	Move Order No. 7. 1st R.G.L.I.		
Heading	86th Brigade. 29th Division. 1st Battalion Royal Guernsey Light Infantry April 1918		

War Diary	Warrington Camp.	01/04/1918	03/04/1918
War Diary	Hamburch.	07/04/1918	07/04/1918
War Diary	Warrington Camp.	09/04/1918	09/04/1918
War Diary	Neuf Berquin.	10/04/1918	14/04/1918
War Diary	St Sylvestre Cappel.	14/04/1918	19/04/1918
War Diary	Hondeghem	19/04/1918	27/04/1918
War Diary	Ebblinghem.	28/04/1918	28/04/1918
War Diary	Etaples.	29/04/1918	29/04/1918
War Diary	St. Aubin.	30/04/1918	30/04/1918
Miscellaneous	1st Bn. R. Guernsey L.I. Casualty List No. 7		
Miscellaneous	Relief Orders. 1st Bn: Royal Guernsey L.I.	02/04/1918	02/04/1918
Miscellaneous	Relief Order. 1st R. Guernsey L.I.	06/11/1918	06/11/1918
Heading	Relief Orders.		
Miscellaneous	Move Orders. 1st Bn: R. Guernsey L.I.	09/04/1918	09/04/1918
Miscellaneous	Special Order Of The Day by Major-General D.E. Cayley, C.M.G. Commanding 29th Division.	24/04/1918	24/04/1918

W0951/2302

29TH DIVISION
86TH INFY BDE

From U.K
1ST BN ROY. GUERNSEY LT INFY
1917-APR 1918
Sent

To G H Q Troops

Sep 1 Oct '17

D.A.G.,
3rd Echelon, BASE.

      Herewith War Diary for the Unit under my command up to and including the 31st of the present month.

31st October 1917.

C.H. Forbes Major
fn LIEUT. COLONEL,
COMMANDING 1ST (S) BN. R.G.L.I.

WAR DIARY or INTELLIGENCE SUMMARY

Army Form C. 2118.

1-10

Place	Date	Hour	Summary of Events and Information	Remarks and references to Appendices
BOURNE PARK CAMP CANTERBURY	26/9/17	3:00 to 9:00	1st Batt. Royal Guernsey Light Infantry marched out for Dover. Western Strength 44 Officers 964 OR. Entrained in three trains - Detrained 10:30 - 14:30 26.9.17	Op. Od. no 1 41 25 7A 26.9.17
SOUTHAMPTON	—	17:00	Unit embarked S.W. Miller and sailed 18:00	
HAVRE	27/9/17	6:30	Arrived Disembarked	
HAVRE	28/9/17 to 29/9/17		Unit in Number 2 Rest Camp HAVRE	
HAVRE	30/9/17	18:30	Entrained Point 1 on the Ham. end. Route followed ABBEVILLE - BOULOGNE - ST OMER - PROVEN	Op. Od. no 2 41 30.9.17
PROVEN	1/10/17	20:30	Arrived PROVEN (INTERNATIONAL CORNER STATION)	

UNIT.	Time of departure from STOKE CAMP.	Route.	Time of arrival at PESELHOEK.	Time of departure from PESELHOEK.	Train.
"B" Coy. 1 Cooker Team.	23.00. 16th.	Instructions have been issued to O.C. Coys etc.	1.00. 17th.	2.30. 17th.	10
H.Q. "A" Coy. "C" " Less 1 Platoon. D Coy	6.15. 17th.		8.50.	10.20. 17th.	12
Transport (Less 1 Cooker & Team). 1 Platoon "C" Coy.	5.00. 17th.		7.20.	10.20. 17th.	12

SECRET   Copy No...19....

1st (S) Bn. Royal Guernsey Light Infantry.

OPERATION ORDER. (No.1)

1. INFORMATION.   The Battalion will proceed overseas on the 26-9-17.

2. INSTRUCTIONS.   Companies will parade as under:-

1st Train load.

"C" Coy.   less R.S.M., 14 Transport Personnel, Pte Hunt (Q.M.R)store, R.S.M's batman and C.Os' batman, Sgt. Everest, Sgt. Dorey and L/Cpl Dorey.

"B" Coy.   less 13 Transport.

"D" "   103 men.

The following officers will parade with this party:-
   Major. W.H.Foote (in Command).
   The Adjutant.
   All Officers, "B" Coy, including 2.Lieuts. Morgan and Andrews.
   All Officers "C" Coy, including Lts. Sangster and Chapman.
   Capt. McIlwraith, Lieuts. Hanson and Dorey.

Total 22 Officers and 550 other ranks.
Parade at 2.30, march off at 2.45.

2nd Train Load.

"A" Coy.   Less 12 Transport, Sgt. Gallienne and Transport Officers' Batman.

"D" Coy.   Sgt. Everest, Sgt. Dorey and L/Cpl. Dorey, R.S.M. and R.S.M's' Batman.

"D" Coy.   115 men.

The following Officers will parade with this party:-
   Major. Davey (in Command.)
   All Officers "A" Coy, including Lts. Dixon, Gribble, and Mitchell.
   Capt. Le Bas, and remaining Officers "D" Coy including 2.Lts. Rawkins, Johns and Stranger.

Total 15 Officers and 342 other ranks.

Parade at 4.30, march off at 4.45.

Smoking
~~Drinking~~ inside the sheds in the docks, or on board ship except on upper deck is strictly prohibited.

3rd Train load.

Transport Establishment including Grooms, Commanding Officers' Batman, R.Q.M.S., Sgt. Gallienne, Ptes. Giles, Hunt, Officers' Mess Sergt, 10 men of "D" Coy.

The undermentioned Officers will accompany the party:-
   Commanding Officer. (in Command)
   Assistant Adjutant.
   Transport Officer.
   Quartermaster.
   Lieut. G.E.F.Borratt.
   2.Lieut. Durand.
   Medical Officer.

Total 7 Officers and 70 other ranks.

Parade at 6.00 march off at 6.15.

All animals, vehicles and cycles will accompany this party. "D" Company signallers will be included in the number of men of "D" Coy in this party and will take charge of cycles.
BANDSMEN WILL PARADE WITH THEIR COMPANIES.

3. DISCIPLINE. (1)   Officers Commanding Companies will arrange to have a responsible N.C.O. i/c of each compartment.
              (2)   No men will leave the train at any halt without leave of the Officer i/c Trains.
              (3)   The voyage across channel will be treated as a night march, and no lights or noise will be permitted.

-2-

UNLOADING PARTY. Lieut. G.F.P.Borrett and 20 men will report to the Railway Transport Officer on arrival. The 20 men will be found as under:-

  10 men of "D" Coy in the 3rd train load.
  10 Brakesmen.

This party will unload the vehicle so as to clear the train as quickly as possible, and after is cleared will drag the vehicles by the cranes detailed by the Embarkation Staff and assist in slinging.

5. **HOLD PARTIES.** 2 parties each of 1 N.C.O. and 5 men will be detailed by the O.C. 2nd Train party and will report to the embarkation officer, for duty in the hold assisting stevedores.

6. **EMBARKATION.** On arrival the Officers Commanding Train loads will immediately report to Embarkation Officer for instructions.

7. **RETURNS.** The senior officer with each train load will render to the Embarkation Officer at point of embarkation, a train state and shortage return.

      (sd) A.F.C.Borrett Lieut.
    Adjutant 1st (S) Bn. R. Guernsey L.I.

Bourne Park Camp,
25th Sept 1917.

No.1	Commanding Officer.
2	2nd in command.
3	Adjutant.
4	Assistant Adjutant.
5	Quartermaster.
6	Transport Officer.
7	Officer i/c Signals.
8	Lieut. G.K.F.Borrett.
9 & 10	O.C. "A" Coy.
11 & 12	" "B" "
13 & 14	" "C" "
15 & 16	" "D" "
17	R.S.M.
18	Medical Officer.
19 & 20	File.

SECRET.   COPY No. ....

1st.Bn:Royal Guernsey L.I.

Operation Order No.4.

1. **INFORMATION.**
   The Battalion will move this afternoon.

2. **INSTRUCTIONS.**

   (a) The Battalion will parade at 16.30. March off at 17.30 for POINT 1 (Entrance No 70 COURS DE LA REPUBLICQUE)
   Detail of march:-
   Headquarters (Fighting Portion.)
   "A" Coy. less 1 Officer and 30 other ranks.
   "B" Coy.
   Drums and Bugles.
   "C" Coy.
   "D" Coy. less 1 N.C.O. and 10 other ranks.
   Headquarters (Administrative Portion.)
   Transport will be drawn up in rear of the Battalion.
   O.C."D" Coy. will detail one Platoon to march in rear of the Transport.

   (b) <u>RATION PARTY.</u>
   O.C."A" Coy. will detail 1 Officer and 30 men who will march at the head to POINT 4 (Entrance as for POINT 1) and report to the Officer i/c Detail Issue Store.

   (c) <u>LOADING PARTY.</u>
   O.C. "D" Coy. will detail at the Station 1 Officer and 50 men to assist in loading baggage and transport on Train.

   (d) <u>BAGGAGE & OFFICERS KITS.</u>
   Two lorries will report at 15.00. All baggage and kits are to be ready stacked by that hour. O.C."D" Coy. will detail 1 N.C.O. and 8 men as baggage guard.

   (e) 2/Lieut.C.H.Manson will proceed with the lorries in advance of the Battalion to take over train and allot accommodation.

   (f) <u>PICQUETS.</u>
   O.C. "B" Coy. and "C"Coy will each detail a picquet of 1 N.C.O. and 10 men to alight at each halt to prevent men from leaving the train. One picquet will be at each end of the train.

   (g) <u>GUARD.</u>
   O.C. "C" Coy. will detail 1 Sgt and 3 men to guard the Refreshment Rooms at Stations to prevent men from entering.

3. **DISCIPLINE.**

   (a) Water bottles must be filled before marching off.
   (b) O.C.Coys.etc. must see that every man is told the station and point of entrainment <u>before marching off.</u>
   (c) No equipment is to be taken off at the station nor are arms to be piled.
   (d) Every man must clearly understand that he is not to leave the train for any purpose whatever without the permission of O.C.Train. Any breach of this order will be severely punished.

4. **STATES.**

   The R.S.M. for Headquarters. O.C. Coys, and the Transport Officer will hand Marching out States to the Adjutant on parade.

   (sd) A.F.C.Barrett Lieut.
   Adjt. 1st Bn: R.Guernsey L.I.

ISSUED AT
   11.45.
   Copy No.1........C.O.   Copy No.6........O.C. "D" Coy.
   "   "   2........Major Foote   "   "   7........M.O.Phelan.
   "   "   3........O.C."A" Coy.   "   "   8........T.O.
   "   "   4........O.C."B" "   "   "   9........R.S.M.
   "   "   5........O.C."C" "   "   " 10........2/Lt.Manson.
   "   " 11........File.

SECRET.   COPY NO....8........

1st (S) Bn: ROYAL GUERNSEY L.I.

Operation Order No.3.

1. **INFORMATION.**

"A" & "D" Coys and 30 men detailed by O.C. "C" Coy will move this afternoon to PARROY CAMP.

2. **INSTRUCTIONS.**

The above will parade at 14.00 and march off at 14.15 for INTERNATIONAL CORNER STATION. They will report to the R.T.O. there at 16.30. Guides will be provided by the 1/2 MONMOUTHS at ELVERDINGHE STATION.

The composite Battalion of H.Q. and 2 Coys 1/2nd MONMOUTHS and 2 Coys GUERNSEY LIGHT INFANTRY will be at the disposal of the C.E. XIV CORPS from ZERO hour and will receive orders from him.

The 30 N.C.Os and men from "C" Coy will be under the A.D.M.S.

DRESS:- Field Service marching order. Blankets will be carried on the man.

The following will be left behind:-
Men on Headquarters, Buglers and drummers.

Only one Officer per platoon will go with their Companies.

TRANSPORT. Companies will take their cookers, and Lewis Guns and ammunition in their limbers.
1 water cart will be taken.
The transport officer will provide two limbers for Officers Kits at 14.00.
The transport will proceed by road to PARROY CAMP.
100 shovels will be carried in another limber.
RATIONS. will be issued for one day.

A.F.C. Bouett
Lieut.
Adjutant 1st (S) Bn: R.Guernsey L.I.

ISSUED AT:- 12.30

```
Copy No.1 issued to O.C. "A" Coy.
     2    "    "   O.C. "D"  "
     3    "    "   O.C. "C"  "
     4    "    "   " Transport Officer.
     5    "    "   " Quartermaster.
     6    "    "   " Regtl. Sergt. Major.
     7    "    "   " Commanding Officer.
     8)   "    "   " FILED.
     9)
```

SECRET.   COPY No. 7

                           1st (S) Bn: R. Guernsey L.I.
                           OPERATION ORDER NO.4.
                                                            16th October 1917.
Refce. Map.
Sheet 27 & 28
Edition 3.

1. **INFORMATION.**   The Battalion will move with the 86 Bde Group to the Third Army Area on 17-10-17.

2. **INTENTION.**   The Battalion will march out from STOKE CAMP on the night 16-17 October for PESELHOEK (A.30.b.8.8.) where it will entrain for SAULTY. Approximate length of ~~march~~ journey 7 hours.

3. **INSTRUCTIONS.**
   (a)   Troops will march in file with 200x distance between Companies.
   (b)   All watches will be synchronised before departure. Companies will halt independently at 10 minutes to the hour until the hour.
   (c)   O.C. "C" Coy will detail 1 Platoon to load ~~thextrain~~ and unload at place of detrainment the train.
         This platoon will march out with the transport.
   (d)   2.Lieut. C.H.Manson assisted by 2.Lieut. A.T.Pirouet will march out with the transport and take over train No.12. O.C. "B" Coy will similarly detail an Officer who will arrive at PESELHOEK not later than 23.30 on the 16th. These Officers will report to the Officer of the Brigade Staff on duty ~~on~~ at the entraining station, and will take with them a complete marching out state shewing the number of men, horses, G.S. Limbers G.S., and 2 wheeled wagons proceeding by the train.
   (e)   O.C. "B" Coy will report to O.C. No.10 train for instructions with regard to Picquets etc.
   (f)   O.C. "A" & "D" Coys will each detail 1 Sergeant and 6 men who will travel at the ends of No.10 train to prevent troops from leaving the train without permission.
   (g)   All doors on the right hand side of the train when on the main line are to be kept closed.
   (h)   Troops will carry rations for the day following the day of detrainment.
   (i)   All Officers' Kits are to be stacked outside the Officers' Mess by 3.30.
   (j)   C.Q.M.Sgts and storemen will travel with their Coys.

                                      (sd) A.F.C.Borrett Lieut.
                        Adjutant 1st (S) Bn: R.Guernsey L.I.

(Time of issue, 13.00........)

         No.1   Commanding Officer.
            2   Major. Foote.
            3   O.C. "A" Coy.
            4   "   "B" "
            5   "   "C" "
            6   "   "D" "
            7   Quartermaster.
            8   Transport Officer.
            9   Lewis Gun Officer.
           10   Medical Officer.
           11   Signalling Officer.
           12   2.Lieut. Manson.
           13   File.
           14   R.S.M.

SECRET.   Copy No 19.
1st (S) Bn. Royal Guernsey Light Infantry.
OPERATION ORDER. (No 1)

1. **INFORMATION.** The Battalion will proceed overseas on the 26-9-17.

2. **INSTRUCTIONS.** Companies will parade as under:-

   <u>1st train load.</u>

   "C" Coy.   less R.S.M. 14 Transport personnel, Pte Hunt (Q.M. store
              R.S.M's batman and C.O's batman, Sgt Everest, Sgt Dorey
              and L/Cpl Dorey.
   "B" Coy.   less 13 Transport.
   "D" Coy.   103 men.

   The following Officers will parade with this party:-
       Major W.H. Foote (in command)
       The Adjutant.
       All Officers "B" Coy, including 2 Lieuts Morgan and
       Andrews.
       All Officers "C" Coy, including Lts Sangster and Chapman
       Capt Mollwraith, Lieuts Manson and Dorey.

       Total 22 Officers and 550 other ranks.
       Parade at 2.30, march off at 2.45.

   <u>2nd Train Load.</u>

   "A" Coy.   Less 12 Transport, Sgt Gallienne and Transport Officers'
              Batman.
              Sgt Everest, Sgt Dorey and L/Cpl Dorey, R.S.M. and R.S.M's
              Batman.
   "D" Coy   115 men.
       The following Officers will parade with this party:-
           Major Davey (in command)
       All Officers "A" Coy including Lts Dixon, Gribble and
   Mitchell.
       Capt Le Bas, and remaining Officers "D" Coy including
   2 Lts Rawkins, Johns and Stranger.
       Total 15 Officers and 342 other ranks.
       parade at 4.30, march off at 4.45.

   Smoking inside the sheds in the docks, or on board Ship
   except on upper deck is strictly prohibited.

   <u>3rd Train load.</u>
     Transport Establishment including Grooms, Commanding Officer
   Batman, R.Q.M.S. Sergt Gallienne, Ptes Giles, Hunt, Officers'
   Mess Sergt, 10 men of "D" Coy.

   The undermentioned Officers will accompany the party:-
       Commanding Officer. (in Command)
       Assistant Adjutant.
       Transport Officer.
       Quartermaster.
       Lieut G.K.F. Borrett.
       2 Lieut Durand
       Medical Officer.
     Total 7 Officers and 70 other ranks.
   Parade at 6.00 march off at 6.15.
   All animals, vehicles and cycles will accompany this party.
   "D" Company signallers will be included in the number of
   men of "D" Coy in this party and will take charge of cycles
   Bandsmen will parade with their Companies.

3. **DISCIPLINE.** (1) Officers Commanding Companies will arrange to have a
                responsible N.C.O. i/c of each Compartment.
             (2) No men will leave the train at any halt without leave
                of the Officer i/c Trains.
             (3) The voyage across channel will be treated as a night
                march, and no lights or noise will be permitted.

SECRET.   COPY No............

1st. Bn: Royal Guernsey L.I.

Operation Order No. 2.

1. **INFORMATION.**

   The Battalion will move this afternoon.

2. **INSTRUCTIONS.**

   (a) The Battalion will parade at 16.30. March off at 17.30 for POINT 1 (Entrance No 7C COURS DE LA REPUBLICQUE.)
   Detail of march:-

   Headquarters (Fighting Portion.)
   "A" Coy.less 1 Officer and 30 other ranks.
   "B" Coy.
   Drums and Bugles.
   "C" Coy.
   "D" Coy.less 1 N.C.O. and 18 other ranks.
   Headquarters (Administrative Portion.)
   Transport will be drawn up in rear of the Battalion.
   O.C. "D" Coy. will detail one Platoon to march in rear of the Transport.

   (b) RATION PARTY.

   O.C. "A" Coy. will detail 1 Officer and 30 men who will march at the head to POINT 4(Entrance as for POINT 1) and report to the Officer i/c Detail Issue Store.

   (c) LOADING PARTY.

   O.C. "D" Coy. will detail at the Station 1 Officer and 50 men to assist in loading baggage and transport on Train.

   (d) BAGGAGE & OFFICERS KITS.

   Two lorries will report ay 15. 00 . All baggage and kits are to be ready stacked by that hour. O.C. "D" Coy. will detail 1 N.C.O. and 8 men as baggage guard.

   (e) 2/Lieut. C.H. Manson will proceed with the lorries in advance of the Battalion to take over train and allot accommodation.

   (f) PICQUETS.

   O.C. "B" and "C" Coys. will each detail a picquet of 1 N.C.O. and 10 men to alight at each halt to prevent men from leaving the train. One picquet will be at each end of the train.

   (g) GUARD.

   O.C. "C" Coy. will detail 1 Sgt. and 3 men to guard the Refreshment Rooms at stations to prevent men from entering.

3. **DISCIPLINE.**

   (a) Water bottles must be filled before marching off.
   (b) O.C.Coys. etc. must see that every man is told the station and point of entrainment before marching off.
   (c) No equipment is to be taken off at the station nor are arms to be piled.
   (d) Every man must clearly understand that he is not to leave the train for any purpose whatever without the permission of O.C. Train . Any breach of this order will be severely punished.

4. **STATES.**

   The R.S.M. for Headquarters. O.C. Coys, and the Transport Officer will hand Marching out States to the Adjutant on parade.

                                  (Sd) A.F.C.Borrett Lieut.
                             Adjt. 1st. Bn: R. Guernsey L.I.

   ISSUED AT
        11.45.
   Copy No. 1.........O.C.   Copy No. 6........O.C."D" Coy.
     "   " 2.........Major Foote   "   " 7........Q.Mstr.
     "   " 3.........O.C."A" Coy.   "   " 8........T.O.
     "   " 4.........O.C."B" "   "   " 9........R.S.M.
     "   " 5.........O.C."C" "   "   " 10........2/Lt.Manson.

(2)

UNLOADING PARTY. Lieut G.F.F.Borrett and 20 men will report to the Railway Transport Officer on arrival. The 20 men will be found as under:-

    10 men of "D" Coy in the 3rd train load
    10 Brakesmen.

This party will unload the vehicle so as to clear the train as quickly as possible, and after is cleared will drag the vehicles to the cranes detailed by the Embarkation Staff and assist in slinging.

5. **HOLD PARTIES.** 2 parties each of 1 N.C.O. and 5 men will be detailed by the O.C. 2nd train party and will report to the embarkation Officer, for duty in the hold assisting stevedores.

6. **EMBARKATION.** On arrival of the Officers Commanding Train loads will immediately report to Embarkation Officer for instructions.

7. **RETURNS.** The senior Officer with each train load will render to the Embarkation Officer at point of embarkation, a train state and shortage return.

                            (sd) A.F.C.Borrett Lieut.
                    Adjutant 1st (S) Bn R.Guernsey L.I.

Bourne Park Camp,
  25th Sept 1917.

No	
1.	Commanding Officer
2	2nd in Command
3	Adjutant
4	Assistant Adjutant
5	Quartermaster
6	Transport Officer
7	Officer i/c Signals
8	Lieut G.F.F.Borrett
9 & 10	"A" Coy.
11 & 12	"B" Coy
13 & 14	"C" Coy
15 & 16	"D" Coy
17	R.S.M.
18	Medical Officer
19 & 20	File.

SECRET.   COPY NO. ....9......

1st. (S) Bn: ROYAL GUERNSEY L.I.

Operation Order No. 3.

1. **INFORMATION.**

   "A" & "D" Coys and 50 men detailed by O.C. "C" Coy. will move this afternoon to PARROY CAMP.

2. **INSTRUCTIONS.**

   The above will parade at 14.00 and march off at 14.15 for INTERNATIONAL CORNER STATION. They will report to the R.T.O. there at 15.30. Guides will be provided by the 1/2 MONMOUTHS at ELVERDINGHE STATION.

   The composite Battalion of H.Q. and 2 Coys 1/2nd. MONMOUTHS and 2 Coys. GUERNSEY LIGHT INFANTRY will be at the disposal of the C.E. XIV CORPS from ZERO hour and will receive orders from him.

   The 50 N.C.Os and men from "C" Coy. will be under the A.D.M.S.

   DRESS:- Field Service marching order. Blankets will be carried on the man.

   The following will be left behind:-
   Men on Headquarters, Buglers and drummers.

   Only one Officer per platoon will go with their Companies.

   TRANSPORT. Companies will take their cookers, and Lewis Guns and ammunition in their limbers.
   1 water cart will be taken.
   The Transport Officer will provide two limbers for Officers Kits at 14.00.
   The Transport will proceed by road to PARROY CAMP.
   100 shovels will be carried in another limber.
   RATIONS, will be issued for one day.

   (Sd) A.F.C. Borrett Lieut.
   Adjutant 1st. (S) Bn: R. Guernsey L.I.

   ISSUED AT:- 12.30

   Copy No. 1 issued to O.C. "A" Coy.
        2   "   " O.C. "D" Coy.
        3   "   " O.C. "C" Coy.
        4   "   " Transport Officer.
        5   "   " Quartermaster.
        6   "   " Regtl. Sergt. Major.
        7   "   " Commanding Officer.
        8)   "   " FILED.
        9)

Army Form C. 2118.

WAR DIARY
or
INTELLIGENCE SUMMARY
(Erase heading not required.)

Instructions regarding War Diaries and Intelligence Summaries are contained in F.S. Regs., Part II. and the Staff Manual respectively. Title Pages will be prepared in manuscript.

Place	Date	Hour	Summary of Events and Information	Remarks and references to Appendices
STOKE CAMP (F.5 d.1.6)	2/10/17	00.30	Arrived - attached 29TH DIVISION. (XIV CORPS 5TH ARMY)	
STOKE CAMP (F.5 d.1.6) to 6/10/17	2/10/17		Unit in Stoke camp in XIV CORPS AREA - Inspection by MAJ-GENL SIR H. de B. DELISLE cmdg 29th Divn	
	6/10/17		ATTACHMENTS FOR DUTY	
			14 Signallers attached 29TH DIVN SIG COY R.E.	Sgt oral No 2 Sig-10-17
			50 O.R. 'C' Coy attached A.D.M.S. 29TH-DIVN	
			'A' Coy (Strength 189) attached 1/2 Bn. MONMOUTHS (PIONEERS)	
			'D' Coy (Strength 194) attached 1/2 Bn. MONMOUTHS (PIONEERS)	
			Ref above - the Signallers were attached to 29TH DIVN SIG COY R.E. and took part in the operations in the vicinity of	

WAR DIARY
INTELLIGENCE SUMMARY

Army Form C. 2118.

Place	Date	Hour	Summary of Events and Information	Remarks and references to Appendices
PARROY II CAMP (B 16 a.9)			LANGEMARCK CHURCH on 91 v 104 October. They obtained further photos on their work from the Br. 216 Coy RE	
			(2) The 50 O.R. 'C' Coy were employed on Stretcher bearers in the forward battle area 9th – 14th October.	
			(3) 'A' & 'D' Coys attached to 1/2 Monmouths were stationed in PARROY II CAMP near FLERZENBUSH. They proceeded daily to the vicinity of LANGEMARCK and beyond for work on the roads on forward areas from 9th to 14th October.	
			CASUALTIES 'A' Coy KILLED MAJOR A.H.P. DAVEY	
				One O.R.
				WOUNDED 2/LIEUT R.R. MITCHELL Slightly (duty)
				10 O.R.
				MISSING 3 O.R. (Believed Killed)

WAR DIARY
or
INTELLIGENCE SUMMARY

(Erase heading not required.)

Army Form C. 2118.

Instructions regarding War Diaries and Intelligence Summaries are contained in F. S. Regs., Part II. and the Staff Manual respectively. Title Pages will be prepared in manuscript.

Place	Date	Hour	Summary of Events and Information	Remarks and references to Appendices
			CASUALTIES (Continued)	
			'D' Coy WOUNDED O.R. 7	Casualty list no. 1
STOKE CAMP (F.5.d.1.6)	15/10/17	10 am	All detached details rejoined unit.	
—	17/10/17	6 pm	29 Divn proceeded to VI Corps AREA around ARRAS and is attached to 3rd ARMY.	O/o ord. No. 1 d/16.10.17
			This unit proceeded on per maps to PELET HOEK STATION (A.26.b.)	
PELET HOEK (A.26.b.)	18/10/17	1:30 am	Detrained	
AERO NORZ (Q.24.c.2.)	18/10/17	8 am	Detrained and marched to camp.	
HENDECOURT (X.7.a.4.6)	18/10/17	5 pm	Arrived HENDECOURT no. 4 CAMP (X.17.a.4.6) in VI Corps AREA	

Army Form C. 2118.

WAR DIARY
or
INTELLIGENCE SUMMARY
(Erase heading not required.)

Instructions regarding War Diaries and Intelligence Summaries are contained in F. S. Regs., Part II and the Staff Manual respectively. Title Pages will be prepared in manuscript.

Place	Date	Hour	Summary of Events and Information	Remarks and references to Appendices
HENCOURT (X.17.a.4.6)	19/10/17 to 31/10/17		In Divisional Rest. – Programme of training carried out in mornings – in afternoons sports –	
—	30/10/17	7.30	Draft of 240 men from 2nd (Res) B'n R. Sussex L.I. arrived en route from Depot Training Area. accomodated night 30/31" 10/17	

Lt. Col.
Commanding
2nd Royal Sussex Rifle Reg't

SECRET.   COPY No. 13

1st (S) Bn: R. Guernsey L.I.

OPERATION ORDER NO.4.

Refce. Map: 16th October 1917.
Sheet 57 & 58
Edition 3.

1. **INFORMATION.** The Battalion will move with the 86 Bde Group to the Third Army Area on 17-10-17.

2. **INTENTION.** The Battalion will march out from STOKE CAMP on the night 16-17 October for PEBELHOEK (A.30.b.5.5.) where it will entrain for SAULTY. Approximate ~~length of march~~ 7 hours. *length of journey*

3. **INSTRUCTIONS.**

   (a) Troops will march in file with 200^x distance between Companies.

   (b) All watches will be synchronised before departure. Companies will halt independently at 10 minutes to the hour until the hour.

   (c) O.C. "C" Coy will detail 1 Platoon to load Maxims and unload at place of detrainment the train.
   This platoon will march out with the transport.

   (d) 2.Lieut. G.H.Manson assisted by 2.Lieut. A.T.Picquet will march out with the transport and take over train No.12. O.C. "B" Coy will similarly ~~have~~ *detail* an Officer who will arrive at PEBELHOEK not later than 23.30 on the 16th. These Officers will report to the Officer of the Brigade Staff on duty on *at* the entraining station, and will take with them a complete marching out state shewing the number of men, horses, G.S. Limbers G.S., and 2 wheeled wagons proceeding by the train.

   (e) O.C. "B" Coy will report to O.C. No.12 train for instructions with regard to Picquets etc.

   (f) O.C. "A" & "D" Coys will each detail 1 Sergeant and 6 men who will travel at the ends of No.12 train to prevent troops from leaving the train without permission.

   (g) All doors on the right hand side of the train when on the main line are to be kept closed.

   (h) Troops will carry rations for the day following the day of detrainment.

   (i) All Officers' Kits are to be stacked outside the Officers' Mess by 3.30.

   (j) C.Q.M.Sgts and storemen will travel with their Coys.

                                      (sd) A.F.C.Borrett Lieut.
                              Adjutant 1st (S) Bn: R.Guernsey L.I.

(Time of issue. 13.00)

        No.1   Commanding Officer.
           2   Major. Foots.
           3   O.C. "A" Coy.
           4   "   "B" "
           5   "   "C" "
           6   "   "D" "
           7   Quartermaster.
           8   Transport Officer.
           9   Lewis Gun Officer.
          10   Medical Officer.
          11   Signalling Officer.
          12   2.Lieut. Manson.
          13   File.
          14   R.S.M.

1ST (S) BN. R. GUERNSEY. L.I.

Casualty List No 1.

Regtl No.	Rank	Name		Coy	Casualty	Date	Remarks
1076	Pte	Hamon	E.E.	"A"	Wounded	10-10-17	Slight
1201	"	Renouf	A.H.	"	do	do	-do-
399	"	Le Moigne	J.	"	do	do	-do-
1199	"	Godfrey	N.J.	"	do	do	-do-
1043	"	Le Messurier	P.	"	do	do	-do-
1035	"	Gallienne	J.	"	do	do	-do-
596	L/Cpl	Pike	H.	"D"	do	do	-do-
943	Pte	Roberts	J.	"	do	do	-do-
791	"	Roberts	J.H.	"	do	do	-do-
284	"	Pheton	O.P.M.	"	do	do	Serious
993	"	Gallienne	J.	"	do	11-10-17	-do-
867	"	Hewlett	W.E.	"	do	do	Slight
926	"	Fallaize	F.	"	do	do	-do-
	Major	Davey	A.H.P.	"A"	Killed in action	14-10-17	
	Lieut	Mitchell	J.R.	"	Wounded	-do-	
22	Pte	Bourgaize	J.	"	Killed in action	-do-	
571	"	Cataroche	J.	"	Wounded	-do-	Slight
218	"	Le Poury	A.C.	"	-do-	-do-	-do-
81	"	Battle	A.	"	-do-	-do-	-do-
201799	"	Reed	J.E.	"	-do-	-do-	Serious
470	"	Guille	P.	"	Missing	-do-	
213	"	Le Poidevin	W.H.	"	believed killed	-do-	
565	"	Slimm	J.	"		-do-	

21/10/17

W.H.H——, Major for
Lt.Col commdg Royal Guernsey
Light Infantry

1st (S) Bn. R. GUERNSEY. L.I.

Casualty List No 1

Regtl No.	Rank	Name		Coy	Casualty	Date	Remarks
1076	Pte	Hamon	C.E.	A	Wounded	10-10-17	Slight
1201	"	Renouf	A.E.	"	do	do	do
599	"	Le Poidevin	J.	"	do	do	do
1199	"	Godfrey	A.F.	"	do	do	do
1043	"	Le Messurier	P.	"	do	do	do
1035	"	Gallienne	J.	"	do	do	do
896	L/Cpl	Price	H.	B	do	do	do
943	Pte	Roberts	J.	"	do	do	do
791	"	Roberts	J.H.	"	do	do	do
234	"	Phelan	C.P.H.	"	do	do	Serious
443	"	Gallienne	J.	"	do	4-10-17	do
567	"	Hewlett	L.E.	"	do	do	Slight
926	"	Tollage	F.	"	do	do	do
	Major	Kelly	W.H.P.		Killed in action	14-10-17	
	Lieut	Mitchell	F.R.		Wounded	do	
22	Pte	Bourgaize	L.		Killed in action	do	
871	"	Cattroche	J.		Wounded	do	Slight
215	"	Le Poury	C.C.		do	do	do
81	"	Batiste	A.		do	do	do
201799	"	Reid	D.E.		do	do	Serious
490	"	Gaudion	F.		Missing	do	
223	"	Le Poidevin	W.H.		Wounded	do	
565	"	Hamon	J.		Killed	do	

C.H. Stroble
Major for
Lt.Col. cmdg
1st Royal Guernsey Light
Infantry.

21/10/17

SECRET

WAR DIARY.

1 RGLI 86/29
Vol I

Supplements
W.D.

ORDERLY ROOM
No.............
5 NOV 1917
1ST (S) BATTALION
ROYAL GUERNSEY L.I.

Army Form C. 2118.

WAR DIARY
or
INTELLIGENCE SUMMARY
(Erase heading not required.)

Instructions regarding War Diaries and Intelligence Summaries are contained in F. S. Regs, Part II. and the Staff Manual respectively. Title Pages will be prepared in manuscript.

Place	Date	Hour	Summary of Events and Information	Remarks and references to Appendices
BOURNE PARK CAMP (CANTERBURY)	26/9/17	3.30 to 9.00	1st Batt: Royal Fusiliers left Infantry marked out for France. Entrained in the train L.S. Detrained 10.30 - 10.30. 26.9.17	Op. Ord no 1 d/25.9.17
SOUTHAMPTON	27/9/17	17.00	Unit embarked S.W. MILLER and sailed 18 in	
HAVRE	27/9/17	6.30	Arrived Disembarked	
HAVRE	28/9/17 to 29/9/17		Unit in Route 2 Rest Camp Havre	
HAVRE	30/9/17	18.00	Entrained Point 1 in one train-load Route followed ABBÉVILLE - BOULOGNE - ST OMER - PROVEN	Op. Ord no 2 d/30/9
PROVEN	1/9/17	22.30	Arrived PROVEN (INTERNATIONAL CORNER STATION)	

2449 Wt. W14957/M90 750,000 1/16 J.B.C. & A. Forms/C.2118/12.

Army Form C. 2118.

WAR DIARY
or
INTELLIGENCE SUMMARY
(Erase heading not required.)

Place	Date	Hour	Summary of Events and Information	Remarks and references to Appendices
STOKE CAMP (Fd.D.i.6)	24/4/17	00.30	Arrived - Attached 24th Division (XIV Corps 5th Army)	
STOKE CAMP (Fd.D.i.6)	2/5/17 to 6/5/17		Unit in Stoke Camp. Attached 24th Division (XIV Corps Area) Inspection by Maj-Genl Sir H.A.R. Deluré cmdg 24th Divn	
	8/5/17		ATTACHMENTS FOR DUTY Attached 24th Divn Sig Coy RA H. Signallers Lieut A.D.M.B. 24th Divn 50 OR 'C' Coy Attached 1/2 St Mercantile (Punjabis) A Coy (Strength 189) Attached 1/2 8th Mercantile (Punjabis) D Coy (Strength 194)	
			Ref. above - The Strength was attached 8. 24th Divn Sig Coy Re and took part in the operations in the vicinity of	

2449 Wt. W14957/M90 750,000 1/16 J.B.C. & A. Forms/C.2118/12.

WAR DIARY
or
INTELLIGENCE SUMMARY

(Erase heading not required.)

Army Form C. 2118.

Place	Date	Hour	Summary of Events and Information	Remarks and references to Appendices
PATROL CAMP (B 16 e 9.0)			LANGEMARCK CHURCH. On 9th/10th October they obtained a fresh report on their work from the O.C. S/6 Coy R.E.	
	12.		The 50 O.R. 'C' Coy were employed in stretcher bearing in the forward battle area 9th-14th October	
	13.		'A' 'D' Coys started to 1/2 movement were stationed at PATROL II CAMP nr FLANDERN GATE. They provided daily, to the vicinity of LANGEMARCK and beyond for work on the road from 9th to 14th October	
			Casualties: 'A' Coy KILLED RIFLER A.H.P DAVEY on O.R. WOUNDED 2/Lieut P.R. MITCHELL 2/Lt BLOT (at duty) 10 O.R MISSING 3 O.R (Believed KILLED)	Casualty List No. 1

2449 Wt. W14957/M90 750,000 1/16 J.B.C. & A. Forms/C.2118/12.

Army Form C. 2118.

WAR DIARY
or
INTELLIGENCE SUMMARY
(Erase heading not required.)

Instructions regarding War Diaries and Intelligence Summaries are contained in F. S. Regs., Part II. and the Staff Manual respectively. Title Pages will be prepared in manuscript.

Place	Date	Hour	Summary of Events and Information	Remarks and references to Appendices
STORE CAMP (F.d.16)	15/9/17	10 am	CASUALTIES (Continued) "D" Coy WOUNDED O.R. 7	Casualty List no 7
(F.d.16)	2/10/17	6 pm	All detailed details mob movement unit. 29 Div proceeded to VI Corps AREA around ARRAS and was attached to 3rd ARMY. This unit proceeded in [?] in for... to PETELINCK STATION (A.26.b)	
PETELINCK (A.26.b)	3/10/17	12:00	Entrained	
ARRAS (Q.24.b.2)	16/10/17	8 am	Detrained and marched to camp	
HENUICOURT (X.17 a 4.6)	16/10/17	5 pm	Arrived HENDICOURT no 4 CAMP (X.17 a 4.6) in VI Corps Area	

WAR DIARY
INTELLIGENCE SUMMARY

Army Form C. 2118.

Place	Date	Hour	Summary of Events and Information	Remarks and references to Appendices
Itembe Rock (X.7) + w(D) J+(G)	19/9/17 to 29/9/17		Jn Divisional Rest - Programme of training carried out in mornings + in afternoons sports.	
—	30/9/17	17:30	Draft of 240 men from 2nd(Res) Bn R Inniskilling F. arrived en route to Depôt Training Base.	night 30/9/17 10/17

W.H. Hardt. Major for
Lt Colly ander
R. Inniskilling Fusiliers Depot

3rd Echelon

Herewith War Diary for this
Unit for the month of November 1917.

20-12-17.

WAR DIARY
or
INTELLIGENCE SUMMARY
(Erase heading not required.)

Army Form C. 2118.

Instructions regarding War Diaries and Intelligence Summaries are contained in F. S. Regs, Part II. and the Staff Manual respectively. Title Pages will be prepared in manuscript.

Place	Date	Hour	Summary of Events and Information	Remarks and references to Appendices
Hondecourt	12.11.17		Brigade ceremonial parade presentation of medals to the men by Brigadier by R.O.C.	
— do —	13.11.17		Brigade tactical scheme	
— do —	14.11.17		do as reported	
— do —	15.11.17			
— do —	17.11.17	9.30 pm	Divisional operations practising an attack Left Hendecourt and entrained at Boisleux — and short distance of Peronne at 7 AM. 18 hr arrived at Haitis Allaires at 11 AM.	
Haitis Allaines	18.11.17	7 PM	Proceeded to Lievement, arrived at 11.30 PM	
Lievement	25.11.17	2 AM	Left Lievement at 2 AM, proceeded to Hd Brigade Quarters in position for attack at 6.20 AM	
		2 PM	Gunnel(?) Hale position attacked and gained on (Gunnel Hood) at 2 PM	
Mini Wood	26.11.17	8 AM	Enemy Counter attack from the North which was driven off. Rain more intense at 5 PM	
Inconvey Trenches	25.11.17	2.0 PM	Left trenches and took up line at Bapaume at 7 PM	
	27.11.17		Lt Col Hart-Synnot DSO to own command of the Batt from Lt Col W G Bonhani. Battn moved into the Catacombs and remained til morning 29th	
— do —	28.11.17			
— do —	30.11.17	7 AM	Enemy Counter attack. Batt took up defensive position in the Rue Basso and along the Canal Bank. No enemy infantry attack on the front but considerable artillery activity.	

Latory acct/ad
1st R.S.R.J.

Single Copy

1st (S) Battⁿ Royal Guernsey L.I. (operation)
Order No 6

Refce Maps { 51.c.
LENS 1/100,000
AMIENS 1/100,000 }   17.11.17.

1. INFORMATION   The 86th Brigade will move from its present area on the night of the 17/18th.

2. INSTRUCTIONS. (a) Capt. J.H. Luscombe, Capt. J.G. McIlwraith Lts. Sangster and Norman and 41 O.R. will march by road on the 18" inst to MONDICOURT direct from present billets. Nominal Rolls of this party have been issued to O.C. coys etc & to Capt Luscombe. Orders for the march will be issued by Capt. R. Launceston 16th Middlesex Regt, who will command the Bgde. Party.
Capt. J.H. Luscombe will detail 1 N.C.O. to report to Bde Hqrs. at

v) PERSONNEL   Instructions concerning composition
              of H.Qrs. & disposal of pioneers
              etc. have already been issued
              to Coys. & must be strictly
              adhered to.

vi) REPORTS   C.O. will march with H.Qrs.

                          A.F.C. Borrett Capt.
                          Adjt. 1/R.G.L.I.

Issued verbally to
all concerned at
12.30 p.m.

must be completed by 7 a.m.

III RATIONS ~~Billets~~ A breakfast haversack ration for the 18! ~~etc. On arrival at Boulogne station~~ unit will be carried on the man. The remainder of the ~~Rations for the 19th inst. will be issued~~ rations of the 18' unit will be issued in billets. ~~to the Quartermaster.~~

IV BLANKETS. On arrival at ~~BOULOGNE~~ detraining station coys will fall in and blankets will be collected ~~rolled in bundles of 10 under~~ unrolled ~~company arrangements~~ and dumped by companies. Each coy will detail 1 man to act as guard over its dump.

Party of 1 N.C.O. & 8 men of A Coy (already detailed) will first of all unload the blankets carried on the train & then collect & roll in bundles of 10 the blankets dumped by companies, ~~to await arrival of lorries~~. The unloading party will act as guard over the blankets until arrival of lorries.

Time of Departure of Train   0.28 a.m.
During the march to BOISLEUX STATION
intervals of 200 yards will be kept
between companies, &c.
Regulation halts will be observed.
Lieut. C.H. Manson will report to
Lieut G.S. Dixon (Brigade Entraining
officer) at BOISLEUX STATION at 11.pm
the 17th inst.

(2) On arrival at detraining station the
Battalion will Detrain & will march to
a Camp where it will be
billetted. This movement will
be carried out with distances of 100
yards only between companies etc. Guides
from III Corps Cyclists will meet the
Battalion to conduct it to billets. March

9 a.m. on the 18th inst to act as a guide to take ~~the~~ a lorry to present billets to collect kits &

Rations for the 18th inst will be carried by this party.

(b) The remainder of the Battalion will parade, each coy in its own lines, at 9.15 p.m the 17th inst & will march to BOISLEUX STATION where it will entrain ~~party~~.

Order of march. H. 2 rs. &
       A. coy.
       B. coy
       C. Coy.
       D. coy.

Starting Point. Southern ~~portion~~ end of Present Camp.
Time   9.35 p.m.
Route.   HENDICOURT Rd. junction
      S 7 d 8.9 — Rl. junction
      S 14 a 8.3 — S 9 d 1.5.

Sheet 1.   Copy

1st Bn ROYAL GUERNSEY L.I.
(Operation) Order No 8.
                              19-11-17

Ref. Sheet 57.c.
- - - - - - - - - -

1. INTENTION. The Battalion will move on the
   night of the 19/20th to Assembly
   Area about Q.23.a.

2. INSTRUCTIONS. The Battalion will parade
   each coy in its own lines at 1.30 a.m.
   Order of March.   D coy
                     B coy
                     C coy
                     H.Q. (advanced)
                     A coy
                     M. Gun Section
                     Trench Mortars.
                     Yukon Pack Train.
   Intervals of 100ᵡ will be kept
   between coys.
   Starting Point. X 10 b 6.6
   Time   2. 45 a.

Sheet 2

Sheet 3.

On arrival at assembly area
the Battalion will halt in
artillery formation & in diamond
form as under.

```
            D
            ↑
   B ←100'→ 200' ←100'→ C
            ↓
          ⌣
          H.Q
          A. Coy
          M.G. Coy
```

Each coy will be in Artillery
Formation.

Verbal orders have been
issued for subsequent op-
erations.

3. TRANSPORT. Twenty five pack animals
allotted to Battalion will be
ready loaded by 1.30 a.m.
These animals will march
100' in rear of Battalion until
the position of assembly

Sheet 4.

where they will come under the orders of Brigade Transport Officer. As early as possible after zero hour Battalion Dumps will be formed as near Battalion H.Q. as possible & the Battalion will be supplied by the Yukon Pack Team under the Regimental Sgt. Maj.

4. ADMINISTRATIVE HD. QRS, will move from present area to VILLERS PLOUICH at 4 a.m. 20" inst. The move will be by cross country route. Baggage must be sent forward with The Batt'n Pack Train moving with The Battalion. Personel to off-load these mules may accompany them.

5. Reports. All reports are to be sent to Batt'n H.Qrs (Advanced)

Sheet 5

Coys will report by runner to Battn H.Qrs as soon as they have formed up in the assembly position. This runner will remain at Battn H.Qrs.

6 STORES Signalling Stores, Trench Mortar Battery & all other stores required for immediate use will be off loaded immediately on arrival at Position of Assembly.

            A.F.C Borrett Capt.
Issued at 20.00   Adjt 1/R.B.L.I

Copy No 1. Filed
No 2. To be circulated, initialled
     by O.C.'s A B C D coys.
      O.C. Trench Mortars,
      O.C. M.G. Section
      Transport officer.
      D.M. R.S.M.

D.A.G.
3rd Echelon

Herewith War Diary for this Unit for the month of December 1917.

31-12-17.

E A Dorey Lieut.
ass't Adjutant for O.C.
1st (S) Bn. R. Guernsey L.I.

WAR DIARY
or
INTELLIGENCE SUMMARY

(Erase heading not required.)

Army Form C. 2118.

Place	Date	Hour	Summary of Events and Information	Remarks and references to Appendices
Masnieres	1/12/17		Batt" held defensive positions round Les Rues Vertes and along the Canal Bank.	No Casualty
"	"	9 am	Enemy Barrage followed by strong enemy infantry attack against the Batt"'s front. The attack was successfully repulsed, all positions remaining intact.	
"	"	3 pm	Enemy Barrage followed by strong enemy infantry attack forcing the first line to withdraw slightly from Les Rues Vertes. The Batt" then held the line of the Canal.	
"	2.12.17	12.45 am	The Batt" successfully withdrew from Masnieres. arrived at the Brown Line at 4 am	
Brown Line	"	5 pm	marched from the Brown Line to Ribecourt where the Batt" was billeted for the night	
Ribecourt	3.12.17	9 am	Batt" marched out of Ribecourt and awaited orders in the trenches outside the village. At 5 pm the Batt" marched on to Havrincourt Wood.	
Havrincourt Wood	4.12.17	P.M.	Batt" marched to Lino arriving there at 4 pm when it was billeted for the night.	
Lino	5.12.17	1.15 pm	Batt" marched from Lino to Etricourt where it entrained at 3 pm arrived at the detraining station at 4 am on the 6.12.17 and marched to Honnin.	
Honnin Thouspal	6.12.17 to 12.12.17		Batt" went into billets at Honnin for rest, refitting and training.	

Army Form C. 2118

WAR DIARY
or
INTELLIGENCE SUMMARY
(Erase heading not required.)

Instructions regarding War Diaries and Intelligence Summaries are contained in F. S. Regs., Part II. and the Staff Manual respectively. Title Pages will be prepared in manuscript.

Place	Date	Hour	Summary of Events and Information	Remarks and references to Appendices
Havrincourt	16.12.17	11.20am	The Batt⁰ marched to Etru where it was billeted for the night.	Ref. Move Order 4
Etru	17.12.17	9.10am	The Batt⁰ marched to Le Parcq where it was billeted for the night.	" " " No 2
Le Parcq	18.12.17	9.10am	The Batt⁰ marched to Verchocq where it went into billets as above	" " " No 3
		6 P.M		
Verchocq	19.12.17	9am	The Batt⁰ commenced training.	
- do -	31.12.17		The Batt⁰ still in training.	

Earry tr act/adj for the
1st R.G.L.I.

1st (S) Bn: R. Guernsey L.I.

Move Order No. 1.

Ref. maps. 51.c. 1/40000
Lens II
Calais 13.
Hazebrouck. S.A.

15th Oct. 1917

(i) The 29th Division is to be transferred from the IVth to the 8th Corps commencing 16th inst, and will be billeted in the FRUGES area.

(ii) 86th Brigade will move by march route.
    Dress:- Fighting Order - Steel helmets will be worn.

(iii) Battalion will be billeted tomorrow night in the BOUBERS-SUR-CACHE area.

(iv) The battalion will start at 11.20.a.m. Starting point, cross-roads H.14.B.2.5. Battalion to be formed up with head of column facing WEST at this point by 11.5.a.m. sharp. Order of march Headquarters, A, B, drums and Bugles C, D, Transport. Route will be via FREVENT.

(v) The following billeting parties will precede the battalion:- (a) Lieut. Hawkins and 1 N.C.O. direct to FRUGES area reporting Brigade Headquarters 12 noon tomorrow.
    (b) Lieut. d'Auvergne and 1 N.C.O from each Coy including Hdqrs Coy will report to the Staff Captain at these Headquarters at 10.a.m tomorrow with bicycles.

(vi) All Officers' kits and mess stores to be at the Quartermasters stores punctually at 9.a.m. Blankets in bundles of ten, neatly rolled and clearly labelled, and packs to be stacked at Company Headquarters by 7.30.a.m for transport by lorries. The overcoats of men without packs will be rolled in bundles of 5 and stacked with the packs, also any surplus stores.
    Sick men, excused marching by the M.O. will act as baggage party and travel on the lorries. They will report at the Quartermasters stores at 7.15.a.m. to guide lorries to Coy Hdqrs and load lorries.

(vii) Reveille will be at 6.30.a.m. breakfasts at 7.30 a.m. Dinners will be cooked and eaten on the march. Sick parade at 7.a.m.

(viii) A distance of 200x will be maintained from the Battalion in front. Bn. Scouts under the Asst. Adjutant will act as connecting files if necessary.

(ix) Company Commanders will see that all billets are left thoroughly clean and will report to this effect to the Adjutant at 11.a.m.

G.W. Ealson
Captain
Adjutant 1st S Bn. R. Guernsey L.I.

1st (S) Bn. R. Guernsey L.I.

Move Order No. 2.

Map. Lens. 11.   16.12.17.

(i) The Battalion will move by march route tomorrow to LE PARCQ. Orders of march Hdqrs, D.C., Drums & Bugles, B.A. Transport. Route CONCHE - FILLIEVRES.

(ii) Start at 9.7.a.m. Battalion will be formed up on the main street ready to move off in column of route facing S.W. by 9.0.a.m. sharp. Head of column at the CHATEAU.

(iii) Reveille at 6.50.a.m. Breakfasts at 7.30.a.m. All blankets, packs and great-coats to be ready stacked outside each Company by 7.a.m. The lorries will pack them up there. Three men per Company and a N.C.O. from "D" Company will report to the Quartermaster or representative at Quartermasters' stores at 7.a.m. for loading up lorries. This same party will report the day after tomorrow for the same purpose. They will not travel on the lorries and must be fit men. All officers' kits and mess stores to be at the Quartermasters' stores by 8.a.m.

(iv) Sick parade will be at 7.a.m. The M.O. will send Company Commanders a list of all men in their Coy excused marching. These men will travel on the lorries and will report at Q.M. stores to Sergt. Jones, R. Fusiliers (attd R.G.L.I.) at 8.15.a.m. who will take charge of them.

(v) Iron rations and odd parcels must be either carried in the haversacks or put in the packs if possible.

(vi) Lieut. d'Auvergne and 1 N.C.O. per Coy, including Hdqrs Coy, will proceed by bicycle to LE PARCQ starting at 8.a.m.

(vii) Billets must be left thoroughly clean, Coy Commanders reporting to this effect to the adjutant by 9.a.m.

(viii) Bn. Scouts under Lieut. Dorey will act as connecting files to maintain a distance of 200x from the Bn: in front.

(ix) Dinners will be cooked on the march and will be eaten during the halt from 12.50 to 2.p.m.

Company commanders must get clearance certificates from the owners of their billets and send same to Orderly Room this evening.

Acknowledge.

                                                                Adjutant 1/R. Guernsey L.I.
                                                                                                    Captain.

Copy. No. 1 C.O.
       2 Office
       3 Adjt.
       4&5 War Diary.
       6 O.C. A Coy.
       7   " B "
       8   " C "
       9   " D "
Copy. No. 10 R.S.M.
       11 Lieut. d'Auvergne
       12 M.O.
       13 Quartermaster
       14 Transport Officer.

1st (S) Bn. R. Guernsey L.I.   Copy No.

Map. Lens. 11.   Move Order No. 3.
     Hazebrouck 5.A.

1. The Bat'n will move by march on tomorrow to VERCHOCQ. Order
of march Hdqrs, D, C, Drums, B, A. Transport. Route RUISSEAUVILLE –
FRUGES

2. Start at 9.10. a.m. The Bat'n will be formed ready to move off punctually
by 9.a.m. on the road on which the coys are billeted in column of route, NORTH. Head
of column at D. Coy. Hdq.

3. Reveille 6.30.a.m. Breakfast 7.a.m. Blankets & packs to be stacked outside
Coys by 7.30 a.m. sharp. Lorries will call for these. Officers' kits to be at
Q.M. stores by 8.a.m.

4. Sick parade at 7.a.m. in the School where B Coy is billeted. The M.O.
will send a list to each Coy Commander of the men in his Coy excused
marching. These men and no others, except any detailed by the
adjutant, will travel on the lorries. They will also act as loading party
for each Coy under Coy arrangements. If there are not enough men
for this purpose in any particular Coy, the Coy Commander will detail
a party not exceeding 4 from his Coy. Sgt Jones (R.S.M.) will travel
by lorry and be in charge of men excused marching. He will collect the lists of
these men from Coy Commanders before the Bat'n moves off and will satisfy
himself that only men on the lists are not with their Coys.

5. Lieut. d'Auvergne and 1 N.C.O. per Coy will leave by bicycle at 9.a.m
for billeting.

6. Lieut. Dovey will use the Bat'n scouts for connecting files with the
16th Middlesex Regt in front, maintaining a distance 200x

7. Dinners will be eaten on the march between 12.50 P.M. and 2.P.M.

8. Coy Commanders will send clearance certificates to the adjutant before
the Bat'n leaves, also certificates that billets are clean.

9. Coy Commanders will decide whether their Coys are to wear overcoats. Iron
rations and loose parcels must be put either in the haversack or pack.

10. On arrival at billets Coys will report to the adjutant when they are all
in.

11. Times detailed above will be strictly adhered to.

12. Acknowledge.

                                        J. LEALE
                                        Captain
                                        Adjutant, 1/R. Guernsey L.I.

Copy No. 1. C.O.
       2. Adjt.
       3. O.C. A. Coy.
       4.   " B   "
       5.   " C   "   Copy No. 11. Transport Officer.
       6.   " D   "   12. Office.
       7. R.S.M.   13. War Diary.
       8. Lieut. d'Auvergne.
       9. M.O.
      10. Quartermaster.

Sheet No 2.

Regtl No.	Rank & Name		Coy	Particulars	Date
474	Pte	De Jersey J	A.	Wounded in Action	1-12-17
862	"	Dorey F.W.	"	-do-	-do-
818	"	Dodd A.J.	B.	-do-	-do-
389	"	De la Mare A.	D	-do-	-do-
269	"	De la Mare H.	"	-do-	-do-
1034	"	Falla O	B	-do-	-do-
927	"	Gartell N.H.	D	-do-	-do-
33	"	Heaume N	D	-do-	-do-
383	"	Ingrouille S	"	-do-	-do-
119	"	Jegu R.F.	"	-do-	-do-
829	"	Le Cheminant E	A.	-do-	-do-
622	"	Le Prevost E.	"	-do-	-do-
1043	"	Le Messurier P.	"	-do-	-do-
979	"	Le Page W.C.	B	-do-	-do-
890	"	Le Cras A.J.	D	-do-	-do-
1039	"	Le Lievre L	"	-do-	-do-
1264	"	Le Poidevin L.	"	-do-	-do-
619	"	Le Sauvage E.F.	"	-do-	-do-
106	"	Le Page E.L.	"	-do-	-do-
981	L/Cpl	Murley C.J.	A	-do-	-do-
360	"	Mollett L.	"	-do-	-do-
1260	Pte	Mahy F.J.	"	-do-	-do-
547	"	Marquis H.a.	"	-do-	-do-
834	"	Moore W.H.	"	-do-	-do-
1195	"	Martin C.	B.	-do-	-do-
1048	"	Massey J	"	-do-	-do-
91	"	Moon C.	"	-do-	-do-
500	"	Noyon A.E	A.	-do-	-do-
473	"	Neville W.C.	B	-do-	-do-
413	"	Ogier W.	A	-do-	-do-
123	L/Cpl	Pidgeon W.J	A	-do-	-do-
115	Pte	Patel J	L	-do-	-do-
1291	L/Cpl	Patel C.S.	L	-do-	-do-
482	Pte	Quirié P	D.	-do-	-do-
178	"	Reeve W.H	D	-do-	-do-

1st Bn. R. Guernsey L.I. Casualty List No 3

Regtl No.	Rank & Name			Coy.	Particulars	Date
161	Sergt.	Hotton	E.A.	D	Killed in Action	1-12-17
553	Cpl	Ozanne	P.J.	A	-do-	-do-
1243	Pte	Ferguson	W.G.	D	-do-	-do-
372	"	Guilbert	R	A	-do-	-do-
476	"	Hutchinson	C	A	-do-	-do-
272	"	Jehan	J	D	-do-	-do-
1064	"	Mann	C.W.	B	-do-	-do-
517	"	Meagher	E	B	-do-	-do-
687	"	Rose	G.A.	B	-do-	-do-
936	"	Sarre	W	D	-do-	-do-
880	"	Le Prevost	H	D	-do-	-do-
894	"	Sarre	N	D	-do-	-do-
557	"	Brown	T.A.	A	-do-	-do-
420	C.S.M.	Le Galley	D.E.	C	Wounded in Action	-do-
328	Sgt	Le Maitre	H	C	-do-	-do-
233	"	Martel	T.H.	C	-do-	-do-
319	L/Sgt	Pearce	G	C	-do-	-do-
626	Cpl	Edmonds	G	D	-do-	-do-
1133	Sgt	Sarre	R.H.J.	D	-do-	-do-
1208	Cpl	Stent	S	D	-do-	-do-
772	L/Cpl	Boulain	W	A	-do-	-do-
717	L/Cpl	Lawrence	H	B	-do-	-do-
914	Cpl	Le Page	C.G.	C	-do-	-do-
385	L/Cpl	Mauc	W.G.	D	-do-	-do-
750	"	Lihou	J.D.	D	-do-	-do-
365	Pte	Berryman	A.E.	A	-do-	-do-
953	"	Bourgaize	J	"	-do-	-do-
373	"	Boalet	J.J.	"	-do-	-do-
1030	"	Blondel	H.L.	"	-do-	-do-
570	"	Bishop	S	"	-do-	-do-
543	"	Bourgaize	J	"	-do-	-do-
782	"	Brehaut	H.J.	B	-do-	-do-
405	"	Cann	W	A	-do-	-do-
418	L/Cpl	Collins	R.W.	"	-do-	-do-

Sheet No 3.

Regtl No	Rank	Name		Coy	Particulars	Date
52	Pte	Roberts	J.	D	Wounded in Action	1.12.17
118	"	Ruse	J.W	D	-do-	-do-
125	"	Sarchet	J.F	A	-do-	-do-
807	"	Saltwell	J.	A.	-do-	-do-
73	"	Sims	A.	D	-do-	-do-
632	"	Torstion	E.	D	-do-	-do-
1135	"	Trachy	C.A.	"	-do-	-do-
1187	"	Baudin	F.	A	-do-	-do-
608	"	Walker	L.J.	B	-do-	-do-
651	"	Corbet	H.	A.	-do-	-do-
537	"	Rupp	F.A	D	-do-	-do-
290	"	Smith	A.	"	-do-	-do-
1247	"	LeMoignan	P	A	-do-	-do-
1216	"	Evans	H.C	D	-do-	-do-
930	"	LeGallez	A.	D	-do-	-do-
1597	"	Mauger	A.	A	-do-	-do-
1725	"	Zabiela	A.	A.	-do-	-do-
241	"	Burridge	A	C	-do-	-do-
102	2/Cpl	Burley	S.J	"	-do-	-do-
265	L/Cpl	Cross	R.	"	-do-	-do-
127	Pte	Guille	A.W.	"	-do-	-do-
1045	"	Ryan	J.F	"	-do-	-do-
120	"	LePage	F.T	"	-do-	-do-
454	"	Michem	C	"	-do-	-do-
1131	L/Cpl	Robinson	W.L.	"	-do-	-do-
459	Pte	Robilliard	B	"	-do-	-do-
1477	"	Robilliard	C	"	-do-	-do-
457	L/Cpl	Ringot	A.	"	-do-	-do-
258	Pte	Walden	R	"	-do-	-do-
1063	"	LeMoigne	A	"	-do-	-do-
200966	"	Bruce	C.C.	B/28Bn attd	-do-	-do-
1152	"	Guille	P.	C?	-do-	-do-
403	"	Cousin	P.	A	-do-	-do-
363	"	Bourgaize	J	"	-do-	-do-
83	"	Carré	J.	"	-do-	-do-
840	"	Richer	P.H.	"	-do-	-do-
266	"	Bougourd	C	B	-do-	-do-

Sheet No 4.

Regtl No	Rank & Name			Coy	Particulars	Date
1175	Pte	Gallienne	H	C	Wounded in Action	1-12-17
985	"	Bisson	N.	B	-do-	-do-
366	"	Brehaut	WS.	A	-do-	-do-
217	L/Cpl	Curtis	RJ	N.	-do-	-do-
703	Pte	De Garis	J	B	-do-	-do-
787	"	Gallienne	O.A.	A.	-do-	-do-
112	"	Gaudin	C.	D	-do-	-do-
917	"	Le Page	A.J.	C	-do-	-do-
948	"	Le Huray	J	A.	-do-	-do-
792	"	Le Prevost	P.J	A.	-do-	-do-
316	"	Allbridge	S	D	-do-	-do-
987	"	Bracke	L.A.	A.	-do-	-do-
665	"	Le Cras	GJ	B.	-do-	-do-
668	"	Liron	A.	"	-do-	-do-
1010	"	Manning	H.J.	A.	-do-	-do-
728	"	Macdonald	JW	B	-do-	-do-
153	"	Torode	C.	B.	-do-	-do-
1279	"	Wright	C.	A	-do-	-do-
1089	"	Stuckey	S.	B	-do-	-do-
246	"	Hines	W.	C	-do-	-do-
748	"	Legg	AJ	B.	-do-	-do-
1011	"	De la Mare	L	A	-do-	-do-
~~5164~~	~~L/Cpl~~	~~Wilson~~	~~T~~	~~B~~	~~-do-~~	-do-
299	Pte	Mahy	Fr.	A	-do-	-do-
320	A/Cpl	Allez	J	A	-do-	-do-
779	Pte	McKane	D	B	-do-	-do-
333	Cpl	Corran	P	D	-do-	-do-
833	Pte	Martel	G.A.	A.	-do-	-do-
366	"	Brehaut	WS	A	-do-	-do-
674	"	Cochrane	S.G.	B.	-do-	-do-
1149	"	Gallaize	A.	A.	-do-	20-11-17
397	"	Jehan	C.W.	A.	-do-	1-12-17
266	"	Bougourd	C.	B.	-do-	-do-

Sheet No 5.

Regtl No	Rank & Name		Coy	Particulars	Date
1310	Pte	Allen J.S.	Drap.	Wounded in Action	1-12-17
1319	"	Allett A.J.	"	do	do
1543	"	Bongoned A	"	do	do
1015	"	Bowditch A	"	do	do
1726	"	Bichard R	"	do	do
1489	"	Bond W	"	do	do
1262	"	Boscher F	"	do	do
1322	"	Bott J	"	do	do
1335	"	Brehaut C	"	do	do
1296	"	Burland W.V.	"	do	do
1328	"	Baker H.	"	do	do
1301	"	Bewey A.	"	do	do
990	"	Bouvier H.G.	"	do	do
1222	"	Carré J	"	do	do
1312	"	Caplain A.J.	"	do	do
1032	"	Collins E	"	do	do
75	"	Cohn W	"	do	do
1338	"	Chick A.L.	"	do	do
1316	"	Coshnell E	"	do	do
1121	"	Collivet J	"	do	do
1545	"	Carré T.J.	"	do	do
1386	"	Duquemin J	"	do	do
1143	"	Dunn W	"	do	do
1317	"	Duplain J.O.	"	do	do
1524	"	Duquemin J.P.	"	do	do
1532	"	De la Aulnivie C	"	do	do
1253	"	De Garrisienne H	"	do	do
1340	"	De la Mare A.J.	"	do	do
1490	"	De Beauchamp A.L.	"	do	do
1566	"	De Caris A	"	do	do
1124	"	Durman W	"	do	do
1583	"	De Putron J	"	do	do
1446	"	Earnshaw F	"	do	do

Sheet No 6.

Regt No	Rank	Name		Coy	Particulars	Date
1246	Pte	Ferguson	G.C	Draft	Wounded in Action	1.12.17
1480	"	Falla	D	"	-do-	-do-
1152	"	Guille	P	"	-do-	-do-
433	"	Garland	E	"	-do-	-do-
1390	"	Guillard	S.J	"	-do-	-do-
1391	"	Girard	W.J	"	-do-	-do-
1049	"	Gallienne	P	"	-do-	-do-
1439	"	Guilbert	W.J.	"	-do-	-do-
1136	"	Hallett	J.G	"	-do-	-do-
1220	"	Honey	E	"	-do-	-do-
1466	"	Jehan	A	"	-do-	-do-
358	"	Lelacheur	A	"	-do-	-do-
941	"	Lowe	J	"	-do-	-do-
1325	"	LeSauvage	J.E	"	-do-	-do-
132	"	Le Page	E.J.	"	-do-	-do-
1402	"	LeSauvage	C	"	-do-	-do-
1278	"	Le Page	P.P	"	-do-	-do-
1439	"	Le Chevry	C	"	-do-	-do-
1363	"	Le Cheminant	A	"	-do-	-do-
1176	"	Le Lacheur	J	"	-do-	-do-
1551	"	Le Tissier	W.M	"	-do-	-do-
1393	"	Le Tissier	W	"	-do-	-do-
1194	"	Le Provost	E	"	-do-	-do-
1528	"	Le Paturel	M.J.	"	-do-	-do-
1430	"	Maurice	P	"	-do-	-do-
1375	"	Mahy	C	"	-do-	-do-
780	"	Mahy	A.E	"	-do-	-do-
1080	"	Mollett	J	"	-do-	-do-
1086	"	Mitton	A.J	"	-do-	-do-
1342	"	Norman	W.F	"	-do-	-do-
467	"	O'Neill	H	"	-do-	-do-
1506	"	Ogier	J.P	"	-do-	-do-
1456	"	Pinney	W	"	-do-	-do-
1178	"	Quenipel	J	"	-do-	-do-
1399	"	Quevatre	W.J.	"	-do-	-do-

Sheet No 7.

Reg'l No	Rank	Name		Coy	Particulars	Date
1508	Pte	Roberts	H.C.	Supp	Wounded in Action	1.12.17
1509	"	Rose	E.P.	"	do	do
1445	"	Rogers	J	"	do	do
1563	"	Renault	WJ	"	do	do
1180	"	Robilliard	R	"	do	do
1066	"	Savident	J	"	do	do
1468	"	Smith	H	"	do	do
1418	"	Savident	J	"	do	do
944	"	Berchet	D	"	do	do
1207	"	Savident	EW	"	do	do
1190	"	Savident	J	"	do	do
1433	"	Spurdle	W	"	do	do
1113	"	Smith	H	"	do	do
563	"	Sweet	CH	"	do	do
1558	"	Torode	W	"	do	do
1422	"	Tippell	RJ	"	do	do
1405	"	Taylor	SA	"	do	do
1226	"	Sebert	L	"	do	do
867	"	Hewlett	W	"	do	do
576	Sgt	Bachmann	J	B	Missing	do
587	L/Sgt	Liton	C	A	do	do
773	Cpl	Blondel	CdeG	"	do	do
560	"	LeReverend	A	"	do	do
799	"	Mollett	J	"	do	do
1006	A/Cpl	Perouel	GP	B	do	do
93	"	Falla	WA	"	do	do
1212	"	Price	R	C	do	do
814	Pte	Boutain	JJ	B	do	do
813	"	Bougourd	WJ	"	do	do
628	"	Bressel	RA	"	do	do
1002	"	Carré	WA	B	do	do
939	"	Cornelius	RJ	"	do	do
334	"	Culley	J	B	do	do
490	"	de Carteret	W	A	do	do

Sheet No. 8

Regtl No.	Rank	Name		Coy	Particulars	Date
84	Pte	Denneal	F	A	Missing	1-12-17
992	"	de la Mare	T.	"	do	do
816	"	de Jersey	H.J.	B.	do	do
786	"	Despointes	A	"	do	do
1060	"	Domaille	E	"	do	do
1014	"	Dunn	C.W.	"	do	do
225	"	Flageul	C	A	do	do
658	"	Edmonds	A.R.	B	do	do
1256	"	Furbache	J	"	do	do
1219	"	Frampton	E.J.	"	do	do
345	"	Gaudion	C	"	do	do
890	"	Girard	C.J.	"	do	do
1083	"	Gallienne	J	B	do	do
1036	"	Gallienne	W.H.	B	do	do
35	"	Galliott	H.C.	"	do	do
570	"	Gallienne	S	D	do	do
633	"	Hardwick	C.F.	A	do	do
1181	"	Hubert	C.J.	B.	do	do
908	"	Hudson	P	"	do	do
1019	"	Ingrouille	C.J.	A.	do	do
407	"	Johns	C.H.	"	do	do
302	"	Jehan	S	D	do	do
1265	"	Le Huray	P.	A	do	do
559	A/Sgt	Le Gallondec	E.C.	"	do	do
766	Pte	Langlois	H.	"	do	do
219	"	Le Page	W.J.	"	do	do
69	"	Le Compillot	A	B	do	do
1164	"	Le Huray	E.S.	B	do	do
949	"	Le Tissier	S.H.	"	do	do
574	"	Le Page	W	"	do	do
501	"	Mahent	A	A	do	do
195	"	Merges	W.C.	"	do	do
957	"	Machon	C	B	do	do
1304	"	Mahy	T.J.	"	do	do

Sheet No 9

Regtl No	Rank	Name			Particulars	Date
729	Pte	Martel	E	B	Missing	1-12-17
573	"	Martel	LJ	"	do	do
709	"	Marquand	JH	"	do	do
843	"	Murley	AE	"	do	do
344	"	Mahieu	FJ	D	do	do
852	"	Ogier	W	A	do	do
613	"	Ozanne	H	D	do	do
482	"	Prevel	H	A	do	do
549	"	Queripel	J	"	do	do
803	"	Queripel	WJ	"	do	do
961	"	Queripel	J	"	do	do
730	"	Queripel	J	B	do	do
1108	"	Queripel	J	"	do	do
742	"	Queripel	WJ	"	do	do
224	L/Cpl	Robilliard	LA	A	do	do
1196	Pte	Rolls	F	"	do	do
962	"	Robin	E	B	do	do
964	"	Smith	CS	A	do	do
1068	"	Sohan	FPM	"	do	do
1109	"	Sebire	J	"	do	do
679	"	Sarre	P	B	do	do
1008	"	Sarre	P	B	do	do
678	"	Stagg	R	"	do	do
353	"	Tostevin	W	A	do	do
965	"	Trehon	F	"	do	do
693	"	Vernon	R	B	do	do
1138	"	Warren	JJ	A	do	do
770	"	Walsh	FJ	B	do	do
695	"	West	HJ	B	do	do
1234	"	Downes	EF	D	do	do
1582	"	Elliott	A	D	do	do
64	"	Pengelley	H	D	do	do
184	"	Clark	A	B	do	do
784	"	Caiphas	A	B	do	do
1001	"	Le Messurier	A	B	Missing	do

Sheet No 10.

Regtl No.	Rank & Name			Coy	Particulars	Date
86	Pte	Le Cheminant	H	D	Missing	1.12.17
968	"	Tullier	J	"	-do-	-do-
1408	"	Sarre	M.T.	A	-do-	-do-
689	"	Serre	C.L.	"	-do-	-do-
1091	"	Jowde	W.	"	-do-	-do-
511	"	Bray	L.	B	-do-	-do-
1299	"	Redhead	J.G.	"	-do-	-do-
1292	"	Jardival	E	"	-do-	-do-
158	"	Le Roi	J	"	-do-	-do-
785	"	Chemming	M.J	D	-do-	-do-
959	"	Taylor	W.	"	-do-	-do-
201920	"	Latham	E	3/4 Buff attd	-do-	-do-
642	"	Clancy	A.	C	-do-	-do-
294	"	Roberts	J.H.	"	-do-	-do-
1105	"	Snell	G.E.	"	-do-	-do-
1184	"	Syvret	F.	"	-do-	-do-
1284	"	Welsh	T	"	-do-	-do-
1390	"	Fairbrake	T	"	-do-	-do-
201627	"	Dennee	A	3/4 Buff attd	-do-	-do-
677	L/Cpl	Sharp	G	B	-do-	-do-
310	Pte	Collings	H	A	-do-	-do-
1274	"	Bourgaize	E.J.	"	-do-	-do-
440	"	Hellion	J	C	-do-	-do-
94	"	Hooper	J	C	-do-	-do-
444	"	Le Sauvage	T.	C	-do-	-do-
512	"	Roberts	J.W.	A	-do-	-do-
1110	"	Snell	G.R.	B	-do-	-do-
734	"	Jowde	M.G.	B	-do-	-do-
912	"	Le Maitre	Fr.	A	-do-	-do-
298	"	Rivers	A.A.	A	-do-	-do-
1140	"	Hervé	A.	C	-do-	-do-
236	"	Harris	R.	C	-do-	-do-

Sheet No 11.

Regt No.	Rank	Name			Particulars	Date
969	Pte	Arthur	R	Draft	Missing	1-12-17
1353	"	Allen	AS	"	do	do
528	"	Ashelford	E	"	do	do
859	"	Arthur	P	"	do	do
1336	"	Burnell	RA	"	do	do
1544	"	Bougourd	WH	"	do	do
1504	"	Brehaut	F	"	do	do
1329	"	Baker	J	"	do	do
1410	"	Blatchford	F	"	do	do
1311	"	Benwell	W	"	do	do
18	"	Bishop	E	"	do	do
1119	"	Brouard	W	"	do	do
20	"	Bougourd	G	"	do	do
1500	"	Bell	CH	"	do	do
1283	"	Brehaut	FE	"	do	do
1356	"	Blampied	J	"	do	do
1444	"	Brake	WE	"	do	do
1448	"	Bourgaize	J	"	do	do
1355	"	Bisson	HO	"	do	do
1354	"	Batiste	W	"	do	do
350	"	Brehaut	P	"	do	do
1492	"	Cauvin	P	"	do	do
1057	"	Carré	W	"	do	do
1406	"	Coles	E	"	do	do
1315	"	Coxhill	B	"	do	do
1432	"	Cohu	W	"	do	do
1339	"	Callaway	HE	"	do	do
846	"	Dorey	W	"	do	do
490	"	le Carteret	W	"	do	do
1469	"	le Carteret	H	"	do	do
1479	"	Desperques	F	"	do	do
144	"	Dyke	W	"	do	do
877	"	Dorey	AJ	"	do	do
1315	"	le Lukna	B	"	do	do

Sheet No. 12.

Regtl No	Rank & Name			Coy	Particulars	Date
1282	Pte	Dunstan	J	Depot	Missing	1.12.17
1288	"	Dyke	W	"	do	do
1203	"	Davies	AE	"	do	do
1576	"	de la Mare	W	"	do	do
1566	"	De Caris	A	"	do	do
1383	"	De Caris	F.H	"	do	do
1549	"	De Jausserand	A	"	do	do
1522	"	Duport	H	"	do	do
1122	"	de la Rue	E	"	do	do
1412	"	Edwards	W	"	do	do
371	"	Eborall	E	"	do	do
163	"	Fertracke	W	"	do	do
1349	"	Frampton	WH	"	do	do
1302	"	Farnham	G	"	do	do
1536	"	Falla	W	"	do	do
1360	"	Gorelle	C	"	do	do
864	"	Guille	C	"	do	do
1414	"	Gaudin	B.T	"	do	do
1289	"	Guilbert	J	"	do	do
1357	"	Girard	L	"	do	do
1459	"	Gallienne	G	"	do	do
1157	"	Gallienne	T	"	do	do
1012	"	Cavey	T	"	do	do
1371	"	Hudson	FW	"	do	do
1526	"	Henry	J	"	do	do
1415	"	Hewlett	W	"	do	do
1331	"	Huelin	CA	"	do	do
231	"	LeMuray	HE	"	do	do
1250	"	LeSauvage	G	"	do	do
1364	"	Le Cheminant	LeP	"	do	do
63	"	Le Lachem	L	"	do	do
1365	"	Le Conte	J	"	do	do
1483	"	Lihou	DW	"	do	do

Sheet No 13.

Regtl No.	Rank & Name		Coy	Particulars	Date
1439	Pte	Le Mury C	Draft	Missing	1-12-17
210	"	Lethuay H	"	do	do
1511	"	Lethuay A E	"	do	do
827	"	Le Ber P	"	do	do
243	"	Lacey E	"	do	do
1428	"	Laine J P	"	do	do
199	"	Le Roi A	"	do	do
1421	"	Matthews J V	"	do	do
411	"	Mudge B	"	do	do
1052	"	Morvan P	"	do	do
1389	"	Marsh S W	"	do	do
1065	"	Mollett W	"	do	do
74	"	Marie L	"	do	do
942	"	Maby E	"	do	do
1470	"	Martin P	"	do	do
282	"	Nicholson H	"	do	do
1394	"	Ogier N	"	do	do
1191	"	Ogier F	"	do	do
781	"	Ozanne J	"	do	do
1398	"	Ozanne P H	"	do	do
387	"	Ogier R J	"	do	do
801	"	Priaulx H H	"	do	do
1087	"	Rabey W	"	do	do
1507	"	Roberts G	"	do	do
1369	"	Roberts H	"	do	do
1088	"	Roberts M	"	do	do
1461	"	Reed F	"	do	do
1089	"	Roberts P O	"	do	do
1179	"	Roberts H	"	do	do
1510	"	Simon A J	"	do	do

Sheet No 14.

Reg'tl No	Rank	Name		Coy	Particulars	Date
1471	Pte	Sprackling	T.G	Depot	Missing	1-12-17
1476	"	Stern	J.D	"	do	do
1452	"	Sarre	J	"	do	do
1425	"	Tostevin	A.J	"	do	do
1423	"	Tostevin	W.J	"	do	do
1454	"	Torode	J	"	do	do
1441	"	Thoume	L	"	do	do
1221	"	Trebert	A	"	do	do
1790	"	Sibert	W	"	do	do 600
1111	"	Vidamour	A	"	do	do
1395	"	Welch	E.B	"	do	do
1426	"	Wellbridge	R	"	do	do
1307	L/Cpl	Jago	A	D	Drowned in Action	2-12-17
828	Pte	LePage	J.T.	C	do	do
581	L/Cpl	Couch	A	D	do	3-12-17

1st Bn. Royal Guernsey L.I.

Casualty Report No 5.

Regtl No	Rank & Name		Casualty
1840	Pte	Eaton J.	Wounded in Action 18-2-18.

(1st/S) Bn. R.G.L.I.   Casualty List No 2.

Regtl No.	Rank & Name			Coy.	Particulars	Date
	2nd Lieut	Laine	J. Le J.	—	Killed in Action	20-11-17
	Capt	Bonell	A.R.C.	—	-do-	29-11-17
	Lieut	Arnold	F.W.	—	-do-	30-11-17
+	Lieut	Gribble	C.H.	—	-do-	30-11-17
	Capt	Clark	W.R.F.	—	Wounded in Action	20-11-17
	"	Falla	J.H.	—	-do-	-do-
	"	McIlwraith	J.G.	—	-do-	30-11-17
	"	Luscombe	J.N.	—	-do-	-do-
	Lieut	Le Cheminant	K.	—	-do-	-do-
	"	Norman	S.P.	—	-do-	-do-
	"	Morgan	L.	—	-do-	-do-
	"	Chapman	E.R.	—	-do-	-do-
	"	Beuttler	J.C.O.	—	-do-	-do-
	2nd Lieut	Howiete	J.K.	—	-do-	-do-
	Lieut	Lynch	J.S.	—	Wounded & Missing	-do-
	Lieut	Bonell	G.R.F.	—	Missing	-do-
	"	Andrews	A.V.	—	-do-	-do-
850	L/Cpl	Palmer	R.J.	H	Killed in Action	20-11-17
70	Pte	Priaulx	A.J.	A	-do-	-do-
575	Sgt	Poole	L.M.	A	Wounded in Action	-do-
592	"	Walden	G.	A	-do-	-do-
577	C.S.M.	Brehaut	J.	A	-do-	-do-
117	L/Cpl	Russel	F.C.	A	-do-	-do-
305	Pte	Chick	C.G.	A	-do-	-do-
1275	L/Cpl	Lowinton	F.A.	A	-do-	-do-
29	Pte	Dennis	W.	B	-do-	-do-
25	"	Dorey	W.J.	B	-do-	-do-
660	"	Dorey	A.J.	B	-do-	-do-
295	"	Leadbeater	J.	B	-do-	-do-
1255	"	Mielle	A.C.	B	-do-	-do-
604	"	Trump	E.	B	-do-	-do-
1172	"	Brehaut	B.P.	A	-do-	-do-
564	"	Lorode	A.	A	-do-	-do-
186	"	Burton	C.W.	C	-do-	-do-
432	"	Gartrell	E.	C	-do- (accidentally)	-do-
255	"	Humphrey	F.	C	-do-	-do-

Sheet No 2

Regtl No	Rank	Name		Coy	Particulars	Date
428	Pte	Carré	A.	B	Wounded accidentally	20-11-17
182	Pte	Le Page	W.	C.	Wounded in Action	20-11-17
1024	"	Madell	H.	"	-do-	-do-
148	"	Torode	P.	"	-do-	-do-
392	"	Prigent	H.	"	-do-	-do-
921	"	Proudham	G.	D.	Missing	-do-
193	"	Livings	H.C.	A.	-do-	-do-
338	"	Phillips	C.	"	-do-	-do-
377	L/Cpl	Grout	L.	D.	Wounded in Action	21-11-17
536	Cpl	Quéripel	J.	B.	-do-	-do-
634	Pte	Alley	J.W.	A.	-do-	-do-
303	"	Gavey	W.J.	A.	-do-	-do-
863	"	Guille	P.	D.	-do-	-do-
686	"	Roberts	J.G.	B.	-do-	-do-
844	"	Thoumine	P.J.	A.	-do-	-do-
306	"	Cleale	H.S.	"	-do-	-do-
524	"	Edmonds	J.	B.	-do-	-do-
164	"	Le Lacheur	J.	D.	Missing	-do-
1024	"	Sauvdent	W.	D.	-do-	-do-
641	L/Sgt	Nicolle	C.W.	B.	Wounded in Action	22-11-17
228	L/Cpl	Duquemin	C.H.	A.	-do-	-do-
492	Pte	Gallaize	J.	D.	-do-	-do-
684	"	Lainé	W.P.	B.	-do-	-do-
1081	"	Ozanne	O.	A.	-do-	-do-
410	"	Priaulx	W.	A.	-do-	-do-
865	"	Roberts	C.M.	B.	-do-	-do-
1213	"	Powell	D.	C.	Killed in Action	23-11-17
325	Cpl	Whitford	E.	D.	Wounded in Action	-do-
452	A/CQMS	Manger	A.	A.	-do-	-do-
65	Pte	Falla	J.W.	B.	-do-	-do-
1161	"	Luscombe	W.J.	D.	-do-	-do-
1240	"	Tostevin	C.J.	D.	-do-	-do-
1082	"	Morin	J.	A.	-do-	-do-
646	"	Dorey	J.H.	C.	-do-	-do-
958	L/Cpl	Davidson	W.H.	D.	-do-	-do-
221	A/Cpl	Ozanne	J.	A.	Killed in Action	24-11-17
899	L/Cpl	Varnham	H.	B.	-do-	25-11-17
203	Pte	Glass	J.	B.	-do-	-do-
195	"	Guillbert	J.	B.	-do-	-do-
138	"	Jeyn	S.J.	B.	-do-	-do-
566	"	Square	C.J.	A.	-do-	-do-

Sheet No 3.

Regtl No.	Rank	& Name		Coy	Particulars	Date
723	Pte	Williams	I.	B.	Killed in Action	25-11-17
1159	"	Warren	J.G.	A.	-do-	-do-
798	"	Nicolle	A.J.	A.	Wounded in Action	-do-
637	"	Battle	J.	"	-do-	26-11-17
776	"	Jehan	A.	D.	-do-	-do-
696	"	Merlet	A.J.	A	-do-	-do-
682	"	Torode	W.E.	B	-do-	-do-
139	"	Jurdival	J.	D	-do-	-do-
1120	"	Chauvel	A.	B	-do-	-do-
615	"	Carré	J	A.	-do-	-do-
1228	"	Bullock	H.	A.	-do-	-do-
223	L/Cpl	Le Prevost	H.	A.	-do-	-do-
1018	Pte	Foss	A.E.	C.	Killed in Action	-do-
437	"	Hough	E.W.	C	-do-	27-11-17
451	"	Mitchell	F.	C	-do-	-do-
460	"	Roberts	A.J.	C.	-do-	-do-
812	"	Blondel	A.	B.	-do-	-do-
480	"	Collonette			Wounded in Action	-do-
1033	"	Falla	J.	A.	-do-	-do-
435	"	Gerard	G	B	-do-	-do-
260	"	Hearne	H.	C	-do-	-do-
124	"	Truffit	G.A.	"	-do-	-do-
685	"	Queripel	R.	"	-do-	-do-
676	"	Watson	J.W.	B	-do-	-do-
1259	"	Butt	G.	B	-do-	28-11-17
5169	C.S.M.	Wilson	L.	A.	-do-	-do-
411	Pte	Priaulx	F.	B	-do-	29-11-17
625	C.Q.M.S.	Howlett	C.	A.	-do-	-do-
309	Sgt	Banneville	A.	B	Killed in Action	30-11-17
607	Sgt	Wicks	F.	A.	Wounded in Action	-do-
596	Sgt	Le Poidevin	A.J.	B	-do-	-do-
318	Sgt	Russel	W.J.	"	-do-	-do-
605	Sgt	Sanden	J.	"	-do-	-do-
670	L/Sgt	Bichard	G.	"	-do-	-do-
180	Cpl	Guilbert	J.	"	-do-	-do-
578	"	Hall	H.S.		-do-	-do-
683	"	Toms	W.		-do-	-do-
659	"	Walker	F.		-do-	-do-
722	"	Wateman	W.J.		-do-	-do-
			C.J.		-do-	-do-

Sheet No 4

Regtl No	Rank	Name		Coy	Particulars	Date
341	Pte	Hewlett	A	B.	Wounded in Action	30.11.17
603	2/Cpl	Gorode	N	"	-do-	-do-
545	Pte	Bliey	AS	D	-do-	-do-
495	"	Eker	A.	B	-do-	-do-
698	"	Farnham	JT	"	-do-	-do-
396	"	Harding	FP	"	-do-	-do-
893	"	Ozanne	AJ	"	-do-	-do-
874	"	Pinchemin	J	"	-do-	-do-
700	"	Pomeroy	PC	"	-do-	-do-
456	"	Quemard	F.	C.	-do-	-do-
179	"	Heaume	A	A	-do-	-do-
931	"	Le Page	JT	A	-do-	-do-
1251	"	Le Page	AJ	B	-do-	-do-
754	"	Brouard	WH	C.	-do-	-do-
653	"	Falla	EG.	"	-do-	-do-
1097	"	Gallienne	TJ	"	-do-	-do-
848	"	Girard	E	"	-do-	-do-
847	"	Guille	JP	"	-do-	-do-
262	"	Harris	C	"	-do-	-do-
1077	"	Hawkins	W	"	-do-	-do-
1098	"	Huelin	W.J	"	-do-	-do-
442	"	Le Cheminant	W.	"	-do-	-do-
1022	"	Le Cras	J	"	-do-	-do-
1107	"	Machon	JC	"	-do-	-do-
552	"	Simon	H	A.	-do-	-do-
892	"	Morey	G	C	-do-	-do-
971	"	Brehaut	FR	A	-do-	-do-
142	"	Bennahek	G	B	Missing	-do-
940	"	Howlett	TJ	B	-do-	-do-
582	"	Mebire	W.	C	-do-	-do-
206	"	Bougard	A	D	Wounded in Action	-do-

WAR DIARY
or
INTELLIGENCE SUMMARY

Army Form C. 2118

(Erase heading not required.)

Place	Date	Hour	Summary of Events and Information	Remarks and references to Appendices
VERCHOCQ	1-1-18		Batt" in training Tus 2.1.18	
- do -	3.1.18		Batt" marched to TILQUES AREA when it arrived at about 2.30 pm. Hqrs were established at AUDENTHUN. The remainder of the Batt" billeted in the villages of LEULINE, ETREHEM & LEULINGHEM.	See Move Order N° 4 attached
AUDENTHUN	4.1.18		Batt" training continued. Attack under a barrage, attack on a strong point practised.	
- do -	11.1.18		Brigade Ceremonial Parade. Lieut Col T.J.A. Hanbland awarded D.S.O. The following appeared in B.M. Orders - The Field Marshall Commanding in Chief under authority granted by H.M. The King has awarded decorations as under - Major J.A. Walshoff Wilson M.C. Middlesex Regt att 17R.I.R.J. 2nd bar to M.C. Lieut L.J. Stone M.C. " H.E.K. Stanger D.C.M. Sgt W.H. Badden W.H. Porchin	
- do -	13.1.18		Batt" paraded as strong as possible for Batt Tactical Linen	
- do -	16.1.18		Batt paraded at 7AM and marched to WIZERNES when it entrained for BRANDHOEK	See Move Order N° 25
BRANDHOEK	16.1.18		Batt went into BRAKE CAMP	
- do -	17.1.18		Batt marched to ST JEAN when it went into HASLAR CAMP	
ST JEAN	18.1.18		Bath went up the line and took over its right sector of the Divisional Front from the 2nd Royal Berks (Front Line) and 1st Royal Irish Rifles (Reserve line)	See operation Order N° 01 attached

Army Form C. 2118

WAR DIARY
or
INTELLIGENCE SUMMARY
(Erase heading not required.)

Instructions regarding War Diaries and Intelligence Summaries are contained in F. S. Regs., Part II. and the Staff Manual respectively. Title Pages will be prepared in manuscript.

Place	Date	Hour	Summary of Events and Information	Remarks and references to Appendices
In the line	19.1.18		Batt. locating the line (see casualty list attached)	
	24.1.18		A & B Coys relieved by the Hants and went into California Camp	
	26.1.18		A & B Coys marched from California Camp to Brak Camp, Brandhoek. See relief orders
			C & D Coys relieved entrained at Wulfe arrived at Brak Camp	
		4 A.M. on 27.1.18		
Brak Camp	28.1.18		Cleaning up and training continued	
	30.1.18		Practice Batt. Ceremonial Parade	
	31.1.18		"	

Jeffrey Lieut.
ASST. ADJT. 1ST R. GUERNSEY L.I.
for LIEUT. COLONEL
COMMANDING 1ST R. GUERNSEY L.I.

1st Bn R. Guernsey L.I.

Operation Order No 1.

1. The 2/R.F and the 1st R.G.L.I. will take over the right section of the Divisional Front tonight 18th/19th inst from the 2nd Royal Berks (Front line) and the 1st R. Ir. Rifles (Reserve Line).

2. The O.C. 2/R.F. will assume command of the front line with Bn Hqrs at W.5.C.1.8. The O.C. 1/R.G.L.I. of the reserve line, with Bn Hdqrs at D.4.D.7.2. Bellevue, advance Bde Hqrs will be at KAA 18 (D.13.2.8.6).

    Boundaries will be as follows:-

    Front line:- W 25.C.1.0 to the track at V.30.A.4.5.

    Reserve line:- The reserve line is at Bellevue.

3. The Battn will go into the line as 4 Coys consisting of Coy Hqrs and 2 platoons each. A & B Coys will be under the command of the O.C. 2/R.F. in the front system, 3 platoons in the front line and 1 platoon in immediate support.

    C & D Coys and 2 Coys of the R.F. will be under command of the O.C. 1/R.G.L.I. in the reserve line at BELLEVUE.

    The residue of the Coys will remain behind at ENGLISH FARM C.27.B Central under command of Capt Hutchinson, they will relieve men of their own Coys periodically in the front and reserve trenches and will be used for carrying up rations.

4. Every man going into the trenches will wear leather or fur jerkins, 2 sandbags round each leg instead of puttees, gum boots, P.H. helmets and box respirators in the alert position, and every other man will carry a shovel, no entrenching tools will be carried.

5. All overcoats, entrenching tools & puttees of men going up the line will be put up in the packs and together with the blankets will be handed in to the Q.M. stores by 2pm today. Packs to be clearly marked. Men who have no packs to wrap their entrenching tools & puttees up in their greatcoats.

    Men staying at ENGLISH FARM will keep their packs and blankets, and before they go up the line will send them back to the QM stores.

6. All men going up the line will take 3 pairs of dry socks. Men at ENGLISH FARM will treat their feet properly before going up to relieve men in the line.

7. All trench stores S.A.A. etc will be taken over by Coys in the line and receipts given.

8. Each Battn in the line keeps 20 S.O.S rockets, Battn in reserve 15 each, the S.O.S signal consists of Red over Green over Yellow.

9. Guides:- Coy guides from the 2/Royal Berks will be at SOMME (D.13.2.5.3) at 6.40pm for Coys going into the front line. Coy guides for Coys going into the reserve line will be at the same place at 6.30pm.

    Platoon guides will be at the following places 1 hour later than the above:-
    Coys going into front line } at BELLEVUE on No 5 track.
    reserve }

10. Times for parade.
    A & B Coys will receive orders from the O.C. 2/R.F.
    C & D Coys parade on the road outside the camp at 6.15 pm ready to move off.
    Coys will move in file with 100x interval until meeting platoon guides.
    Route No 5 track BELLEVUE. The battn must be clear of this camp by 5.30 pm.
    Everything must be left thoroughly clean. Rsgt today will hand over the camp to the incoming Regt.

11. East of BELLEVUE no parties larger than 2 men will move about by daylight.

12. 2 days rations and water in petrol tins will be taken into the trenches.

13. Rev Bn Adjrs, QM Stores & Transport will remain at Brigade Camp BRANDHOEK while the Division is in the line.

14. Coys in reserve line will report relief complete to Bn Adjrs at BELLEVUE.

15. ACKNOWLEDGE.

           (sgd) G.C. Pearson   Captain
         Adjutant 1st R. Guernsey. L.I.

1st Bn. R. Guernsey. L.I.

Move Order No 4.

Copy No. 4.

2.1.18.

Ref. Map. HAZEBROUCK. 5A

1. The battalion will move by route march tomorrow to the THIEQUES Area.
Order of march Hdqrs. D. C. Drums B.A. Transport.
Route FAUQUEMBERGUES — AVROULT — CLETY — CREHEM — ESQUERDES
The battalion will be leading the Brigade and the head of the column will pass the cross roads and RENTY church at 7.30. a.m.

2. The battalion will be billeted in the new area as follows:- Hdqrs Coy and transport at LEULINGHEM. A Coy and Coy Hdqrs and 1 platoon B Coy at ETREHEM. 2 Platoons B Coy, C Coy and D Coy at AUDENTHUN.

3. The battalion will be formed up ready to move off at 6.45. a.m. sharp in column of route on the main road facing RENTY. Head of the column opposite D Coy Hqrs.
Dress:- Fighting order, steel helmets. Box respirators slung over the right shoulder hanging on the left side.

4. The following distances will be observed on the march 100 yards between Coys. 100 yards between battalion and transport. 25 yards between each section of 5 vehicles.

5. Reveillé will be at 5. a.m. Breakfasts at 5.30. a.m.
Blankets, packs and greatcoats to be stacked at the side of the main road near Coy Hdqrs by 6.30. a.m. Blankets to be rolled in bundles of 10 securely tied in three places, and labelled. Greatcoats inside packs. The greatcoats of men who have no packs to be made up in bundles of 5. Officers valises should be at 2.M. Stores this afternoon if possible, if not by 6.30.a.m. tomorrow. 1 Stationery box per Coy may be carried on the lorries. 1 Officers Mess box per Coy will be taken on the Mess cart if delivered at Hdqrs Mess not later than 6.30 a.m. Dinners will be eaten on arrival in Billets.

6. The only men to travel on the lorries, with the exception of a few detailed by the Adjutant or 2.M. will be those excused marching by the M.O. at sick parade this afternoon. They will parade with the kits of their Coys and will act as loading parties. They will be in charge of Lieut Carey. The M.O. will send a nominal roll of these men to each Coy Commander and the numbers to the Adjutant this evening.

7. 2nd Lt. Laine, 2nd Lt Brock, the 4. R. Q. M. S. and Sgt Cocheigne will meet the Staff Captain at Hdqrs 16th Middlesex Regt. RENTY with bicycles at 9.30 a.m. to go forward as billeting party.

8. All billets must be left thoroughly clean. Coy Commanders will send a certificate to this effect together with a clearance certificate to the Asst Adjutant before leaving.

9. On arrival in billets Coys will report to Hdqrs when they are all in.

10. Lt Rawlins will precede the battalion with Hdqrs Scouts with shovels to ascertain that the road is clear of snow.

Acknowledge.

G. C. Pealson.
Lt.
Adjutant

Ref. Maps:
— Hazebrouck 1:100000
Belgium Sheet 28 N.W.
Sheet 28 N.E.1.

No. 15

1st Bn. R. Guernsey L.I.
Move Order No 5.

13-1-18

1. The 86th Bde. will move from the TILQUES area to the relief of the 26th Bde. 8th Division in the front area, PASCHENDAALE sector, between the 15th & 19th January.
Bde. Hqrs. in the front area will be at GALLIPOLI, D.13.D.8.3.

2. The Battalion Transport, less cookers, 1 water cart, and the mess-cart, will move at 7.a.m. on the 15th by march route to the BRANDHOEK area, east of POPERINGHE. The Battn. and the cookers, water cart and mess cart, will move on the 16th by train to the BRANDHOEK area. Probable length of journey 2½ hours. On the 17th the Battn. will move to the ST. JEAN area, N.E. of YPRES, and on the night of the 18/19th into the front or reserve line just north of PASCHENDAALE.

3. Entrainment on the 16th will take place at WIZERNES as follows. The Battalion personnel will travel by a train which leaves at 11.AM. detraining at BRANDHOEK. The cookers, mess cart & one water cart will leave by an omnibus train at 10.AM. detraining at HOROOTRE and marching to BRANDHOEK, the latter will be in charge of Cpl. Ferbrache and will be at the station 7.a.m. sharp leaving here at 6.a.m.. The Battn. must arrive at the entraining point by 9.45 a.m., and will be formed up ready to move off in column of fours on the ETREHEN - WISQUES road by 8.a.m. sharp in the following order :- Hqrs. 'A' 'B' 'C' 'D', head of the column to be 200x S. of the cross roads at W.10.D.8.3.. Dress: Full marching order. Steel Helmets to be worn. one blanket to be carried.
Note:- On leaving the train all carriages must be left thoroughly clean. Coys. must detail parties for this purpose. Men must not leave the train at halts.

4. Baggage:- The second blanket and all officers kits not sent on on the wagons on the 15th will be conveyed by lorries to the station on the 16th and will travel either on the personnel or omnibus train. Detailed orders will be issued later, unless otherwise ordered they will be stacked, blankets rolled in bundles of 10 and labelled, at the Q.M. stores by 7.30 a.m.. One Officer's mess box per Coy. will be taken on the mess cart. They must be at the Hqrs. mess by 9.p.m. on the 15th.

5. Each officer commanding Coys must detail an Officer to inspect every billet and certify that they are left thoroughly clean. The usual certificates that all billets are left clean, and clearance certificates will be rendered to the Asst. Adjt. before marching off. No stores or equipment must be left in any billet. Any salvage stores must be handed in to the Q.M. on the 15th.

6. Sick.
The only men who will not march to the station will be those excused by the M.O., these men will report at the Q.M. stores at 7.45 a.m. and will load the lorries with blankets and officers kits. A sick parade will be held at 3.p.m. on the 15th, all men who think they cannot march to WIZERNES will attend this parade.

7. Lt. Rawlins and 4 Hqrs. Scouts will proceed tomorrow by lorry to the BRANDHOEK area, lorry leaves Bde at 7.a.m. 15th inst.

8. Rear Party.
A Rear party, consisting of Lt. Brock & 6 Hqrs Signallers will go round all the billets after the Bn. have left them, and see that all billets have been left thoroughly clean, and that no stores or equipment have been left behind. Lt. Brock will bring this party in rear of the Bn. in time to catch the train at 11.a.m.

9. On arrival in the BRANDHOEK area, Coys will report that they are all settled in camp.

10. The Divisional Commander has noticed that a large number of dogs are with Units. All stray dogs must be destroyed before leaving the area.

G C Seaman Captain
Adjt. 1st Bn. R. Guernsey L.I.

1st R. Guernsey L.I.
Relief Orders

Ref Map 51 1/10000
      57 SE 1/20000
      57 SW 1/20000

1. The Battn. will be relieved on the night of the 26th/27th January on the right sector of the Brigade front by the 1st NFLD Regt. in the right subsector and the 2/Hants Regt. in the left subsector and will proceed to the BRANDHOEK area. The 1st NFLD Regt. will take over Posts A to C inclusive in the front line with 1 Coy of 4 Platoons (No 1 Coy), the portion of the right platoon in close support with 2 platoons and the portion of the right platoon in the GOUDBERG defences with 2 platoons (No 2 Coy).

The 2/Hants Regt. will take over Posts 10 to 15 inclusive in the front line with 3 platoons, the portion of the left platoon in close support with 1 platoon (Z Coy) and of the left platoon in the GOUDBERG defences with 2 platoons (X Coy).

2. Platoon Guides as follows will meet the incoming Regts. at SOMME, the 2/Hants at 4.45 pm, the 1st NFLDs. at 5.30 pm.

For 2/Hants. Y Coy   1 guide
              C "   2 "   (front line & Coy hqrs.
              C "   1 "   (close support)
              X "   1 "   (GOUDBERG)

For 1/NFLD   W   1
              D   3   (1 his Platoon) front line
              Z   2
              C   1   close support
                                     GOUDBERG

These guides will guide their respective platoons back by No. 5. duckboard track, branching off on the newly laid tape laid at right angles to the track which joins the road near to the aid post MOSSELMARKT. The guides for the close support platoons and GOUDBERG Spur will lead their platoons straight to their positions. Guides for each post in the front line will take over each the garrison of his respective post at the aid post and guide them to their post by the quickest route. Coy commanders will tell off intelligent men for this task who know their way well and they will be at the aid post by 5.45 pm and will keep a careful look out for the incoming Battns. and waste no time in taking charge of the garrisons of the posts to which they are guiding. These Post Guides will report to Lt Rankine at the aid Post who will be in discharge.

3. Coys will march independently to WIELTJE Route VIADUCT X Roads, then by tape to No. 5 track, thence to WIELTJE, keeping as long as possible to the duckboards. Lt Rankine will station a man at the position of the tape with the VIADUCT X Roads - Bellevue Road to guide troops until the last man has passed. Coy Commanders must make their own arrangements for collecting their Coys together before reaching WIELTJE.

N.B. Rations for the 16th will be carried on the man. Dixies
11. will be drawn from the Q.M. on the 15th for making tea
for breakfast and dinner on the 16th. Detailed arrangements
will be made by the Q.M direct with Coys.

12. Acknowledge.

The Battn. will entrain at WIELTJE at 1.a.m. Cookers (one for R & S.L.I & 1 for R.F.) will serve hot tea at the entraining point. Lieut Deuton will superintend the entraining. 30 men per truck. On detrainment the 2/R.F. will march under Capt Powell to 'B' Camp, the 1/R.L.S.I. to BRAKE CAMP.

4. All trench stores etc. will be handed over and receipts obtained, which will be handed to the Adjutant at the entraining point.

The full compliment of tools and petrol cans will be brought out of the line, and every man will carry some piece of salvage. These will be dumped at the end of the duck-board-track and ~~completed~~ ~~handed afterwards to the Adjutant~~ from the N.C.O. & collected later.

5. An ambulance will be at SOMME to pick up any men who are incapable of marching further.

6. Relief complete will be reported by Coy. Commander by runner to Bn. Hqrs. at MALLARD X roads after the last man has passed this point.

G. W. Wilson Capt & adj
1/R.L.I.

25/1/18

Rear HQ

D.A.G.,
Base.

Herewith War Diary for this Unit for the month of February 1918.

[Stamp:
1ST
(S) BATTN.,
ROYAL GUERNSEY
LIGHT INFANTRY.
No. 123
Date 1-3-18]

Sausmarez LIEUT.
ASST. ADJT. 1st R. GUERNSEY L.I.
for LIEUT. COLONEL
COMMANDING 1ST R. GUERNSEY L.I.

WAR DIARY
or
INTELLIGENCE SUMMARY

(Erase heading not required.)

Army Form C. 2118

1 R.G.L.I.
Vol 5

Instructions regarding War Diaries and Intelligence Summaries are contained in F.S. Regs., Part II. and the Staff Manual respectively. Title Pages will be prepared in manuscript.

Place	Date	Hour	Summary of Events and Information	Remarks and references to Appendices
BRAKE CAMP	1-2-18 to 3-2-18		Battⁿ in training. Battⁿ relieved the K.O.S.B.s at ENGLISH CAMP. while in this area the Battⁿ was employed on working parties, which consisted mostly in digging lines of defence and wiring.	See Relief Order
HASLER CAMP	9-2-18 11-2-18		Battⁿ moved to HASLER CAMP, and still employed on working parties. Battⁿ was relieved by 2ⁿᵈ Royal Dublins, and entrained at WIELTJE at 1.30 P.M. detraining at POPERINGHE Station at 4 P.M. when it went into billets.	See move order
POPERINGHE	12-2-18 to 19-2-18		Three Coys of the Battⁿ employed on Trenching and Drawing in the forward area, entraining daily at POPERINGHE Station at 8 A.M. and returning each evening at about 5 P.M.	
EEKE AREA	19-2-18 20-2-18 19-2-18		Battⁿ moved to the EEKE area when it went into billets. Battⁿ in Training. Bde Ceremonial Parade, and presentation of ribbons to the following:- Capt. H.L.E.K. Stanger M.C. Lieut. L.J. Stone M.C. A.Sgt.3 Cpl. Creller M.M. "841 Pte Robin V.R. 06 610 — Stephens C.H. 05.	
- do -	28-2-18		Battⁿ in Training.	

La Grey LIEUT.
ASST. ADJT. 1st R. GUERNSEY L.I.
for LIEUT. COLONEL
COMMANDING 1st R. GUERNSEY L.I.

1st Battalion Royal Jersey L.I.

Relief Orders.

2nd February 1918

The 86th Brigade will relieve the 87th Brigade in the WIELTJE sector to-morrow, 3rd instant. The 1st R.G.L.I. will relieve the 1st K.O.S.B. in English Camp.

2. The Battn. will entrain at BRANDHOEK on two trains leaving at 1.20 p.m. and 2.40 p.m. A, B & C Coys. on the first train. Hdqrs and D Coy on the second train for WIELTJE, and march from there to English Camp. The Battn. will be formed up ready to move off on the road outside this camp at 1.45 p.m., Order:- A.B.C.D and Hdqrs. Head of the column at the end of the road which runs through the camp. Dress:- Full Marching Order, Steel Helmets, one blanket to be carried, great coats to be worn. A distance of one hundred yds (100 x) will be maintained between Coys. Between here and BRANDHOEK Coys will march in fours. Between WIELTJE and English Camp in file.

3. The second blankets will be stacked neatly tied in bundles of ten at the side of the road W. of the Camp by 8.30 a.m. for conveyance by lorry. Officers' valises behind the Guard Tent by 11 a.m. for conveyance by limbers. All Officers' or other kit which is not being taken up, will be stacked in a separate pile at the same place by 11 a.m. This will be conveyed to the Q.M. Stores on hand carts by a fatigue party from the Drums.

4. One Lewis Gun and team of 6 per Coy. will proceed with one Lewis Gun Limber to the relief of four anti-aircraft guns of the 1st K.O.S.B. Lieut. Laine will take charge of this party, which will march to English Camp starting at 9.30 a.m. Their packs and blankets will be stacked with the blankets to go by lorry. They will carry one days' rations. The other three Lewis Gun Limbers will be loaded by 10 a.m.

5. Gun limbers, cookers, one water cart, mess cart, maltese cart, and two limbers will proceed by road under arrangements by the Trans. Officer. Rations will be issued at English Camp.

6. 2. Lieut. Street and 1 N.C.O. and 2 men per Coy. including Hdqr. Coy. will go on ahead by road to take over the accommodation in English Camp, and act as unloading party. They will start at 9.30 a.m. and take haversack rations. Their kits will be stacked to go by lorry. 2. Lieut. Street will also take over any stores from the 1st K.O.S.B.

6. This Camp will be left thoroughly clean, Coy Commanders reporting to this effect to the 2nd in Command before leaving.

7. Coys will report when they are settled in the new Camp.

8. A return showing description of accommodation viz. no of messes, huts, tents, shelters, dug outs, occupied by each Coy will be rendered to Orderly Room by 9.30 a.m. on the 4th inst.

9. C.O. in cld will proceed by the lorry to ??? but will return at night, and will remain at the S.M. ??? keeping up rations every night. Coys will have no other personnel beyond ???

10. ACKNOWLEDGE.

Move Order
1st R. Guernsey Light Infantry   10-2-18.

(1) The Battn will be relieved in HASLER Camp tomorrow by the 2/R.F.'s and will move to POPERINGHE.

(2) The Battn will leave Oxford Road Siding by narrow gage railway at 10 a.m. Coys will be on parade in their lines by 9.20 a.m. sharp ready to move off. On receiving the order to move Coys will march to the station in file, keeping 100 yards interval in the following order. Hqrs, A.C. B & D.

(3) Dress:- Full marching order. Steel Helmets, box respirators & P.H. Helmets slung to be worn. One blanket to be carried. All men will carry the blanket inside the pack, and the waterproof sheet neatly folded under the straps of the pack (standard pattern) with 3" shewing below the flap of the pack. Greatcoats will be worn, with the collar turned down and buttoned up. Canteens will be fastened on the back of the pack. No man's rations or mugs will be visible. They must be carried in the pack or haversack Jerkins will either be worn or carried inside the pack.

(4) 2nd blanket will be carried by lorry & must be stacked at the side of the road by 8.30 am sharp. One light duty man per Coy. will act as loading party for the lorry and will travel on it. The packs of the 4 Lewis gun A.A teams will also go on the lorry. 3 Lewis Gun limbers to convey the guns with the Battn, and transport for the Officers valises, Signal stores, Canteen boxes, Mess stores & Medical Stores will be at the Camp at 8 a.m. everything to go by transport will be stacked at the side of the road at this hour, loaded on the transport directly it arrives by properly detailed parties. One Officers Mess box per Coy. will be taken on the Mess cart.

(5) Reveille 6.45 a.m. Breakfasts 7.15 a.m. No sick parade in the morning. Dinners on arrival.

(6) This Camp will be left thoroughly clean. A party of 3 men per Coy. will remain behind when the Battn has gone on parade to ensure that this is done, & will catch up after. A certificate to the effect that the Camp is clean will be given to the 2nd in command.

(7) Guides will meet Coys at POPERINGHE. Coys will report when they are all settled in billets there.

(8) ACKNOWLEDGE.

G. Nelson, Captain
1st R. Guernsey L.I.

1st Bn. Royal Guernsey L.I.

Move Orders No. 6

18-2-18

Ref. Map Sheet Hazebrouck 5A 1/40,000
Belgium and France. Sheet 27.

1. The Battn. less working parties found by "C" & "D" Coys will move to-morrow to the EECKE area by march route.
   Order of march:- H. Coys, Drums and Bugles, "B" Coy, details of "C" & "D", Transport. These details will be formed into one party under Lieut. Stone.
   Route: ABEELE — STEENVOORDE.
   The head of the Column will pass L.12.6.3.5 at 9.30 a.m.
   The Cookers and Mess Cart will Rendez-vous at Q.M. Stores and proceed by the above route at 8.15 under S/Sgt. Martel.

2. The Battn. will be formed up at 9.20 a.m. in the "Rue de BIBILLARDS", head of the column at junction of "Rue de BIBILLARDS" and "Rue de L'OPITAL".
   Dress: Full marching Order, Steel helmets to be carried under the valise straps.
   Lieut. L'auvergne and 1 Sgt. of "B" Coy will march in rear of the Column with the M.O. to bring in stragglers.
   The transport will be drawn up in the "Rue de BOESCHEPE" at junction of this Street and Rue de BIBILLARDS at 9.20 a.m. ready to follow in rear of the Column.

3. The following distances will be maintained:-
   Between Coys   100 x
   Between Battn. & Transport 100 x

4. Reveille will be at 5.30 a.m. Breakfasts 6. a.m.

5. Lorries will report at   at Q.M. Stores;
   Blankets to be stacked at Q.M. Stores at 8.20 a.m. Blankets to be rolled in bundles of ten and labelled. Officers' valises will be at Q.M. Stores at 8. a.m. for loading on G.S. Waggon.
   One stationery box per Coy. may be carried on the Lorries.
   One Officers mess box may be carried on mess cart of 1st Bn. H. Coys. by 7.45 a.m. Mess boxes to be carried on Lorries.
   Packs and rifles of band will be stacked at Q.M. Stores at 8.30 for transport by lorry.
   The only men to ride on lorries will be those excused marching by M.O. and those detailed by Q.M. or Adjutant. Nominal rolls to be submitted to Adjutant by 8 a.m. Men proceeding with lorries will parade with blankets of their Coys. and act as covering parties.

6. All billets are to be left thoroughly clean. An Officer inspection will be done rendered to Major Wilson at 8.45 a.m.

7. Halts. Bn. will halt 10 minutes to the hour till 1.5 hours and 25 minutes past the hour till the ½ hour. During 10 minutes packs will not be removed.

8. A. C. & D. Coys. will proceed in bull marching order in reverse and drawing in the forenoon meal as usual. [illegible] Jones will be in command of the party. On completion of the [illegible] then Coys. will proceed by rail to GOEKWARK-VEREN. thence by route march to EECKE and STEGNVOERDE.

Strict march discipline will be maintained on the line of march. A bolt limber will be detailed to collect the tools from the Stations.

9. Acknowledge.

E. A. Bury   Lieut.
a/ Adjutant 1 Bn. R. Sussex R.

Copy No 1 issued to   Commanding Officer.
  "   " 2 "   "   2nd in Command
  "   " 3 "   "   O.C. "A" Coy
  "   " 4 "   "   "   "B" "
  "   " 5 "   "   "   "C" "
  "   " 6 "   "   "   "D" "
  "   " 7 "   "   Transport Officer
  "   " 8 "   "   Medical Officer
  "   " 9 "   "   Quartermaster
  "   " 10 "   "   R.S.M.
  "   " 11 "   "   Sgt. in "A" Coy
  "   " 12 "   "   "   "B" "
  "   " 13 "   "   "   "C" "
  "   " 14 "   "   "   "D" "
  "   " 15 "   "   [illegible]
  "   " 16 "   "   War Diary
  "   " 17

WAR DIARY
or
INTELLIGENCE SUMMARY
(Erase heading not required.)

Army Form C. 2118

Instructions regarding War Diaries and Intelligence Summaries are contained in F.S. Regs., Part II. and the Staff Manual respectively. Title Pages will be prepared in manuscript.

1 R G L I

Place	Date	Hour	Summary of Events and Information	Remarks and references to Appendices
EECRE AREA	1-3-18		Battⁿ in training	
–do–	7-3-18		Battⁿ moved to the BRANDHOEK AREA and was billeted at RED ROSE CAMP	See move order No 7
BRANDHOEK AREA	8-3-18		Battⁿ moved to IRISH FARM CAMP and took over work in ARMY BATTLE ZONE	See Move order No 8
IRISH FARM CAMP	17-3-18		Battⁿ relieved the 1st LANCS. FUS. in the right sector of the POELCAPPELLE sector	See Relief order
BELLEVUE	23-3-18		Battⁿ was relieved by the 2nd ROYAL FUS. and proceeded to CALIFORNIA CAMP	See Relief order
CALIFORNIA CAMP	27-3-18		Battⁿ relieved the 1st LANCS. FUS. in the Left sector of the Bde front.	See Relief order –do–
BELLEVUE	29-3-18		Battⁿ was relieved by the 1st BORDER REGT and proceeded to WARRINGTON CAMP for rest and training.	–do–

LIEUT.
ASST. ADJT. 1st R. GUERNSEY L.I.
for LIEUT. COLONEL
COMMANDING 1 st R. GUERNSEY L.I.

1st Bn: R. Guernsey L. I.

Casualty List No 4.

Regtl No	Rank & Name			Coy	Casualties	
957	Pte	White	R.S.	B.	Killed in Action	20-1-18
1146	"	Sebire	W.J.	C.	do	22-1-18
1619	"	Burley	G.	a.	do	24-1-18
1218	"	Hamon	K.	a.	do	24-1-18
72	"	Roberts	W.	a.	do	24-1-18
477	"	De Jersey	P.	D.	do	24-1-18
391	"	Saunders	C.E.	D.	Wounded in Action	20-1-18
87	"	Gregg	W.J.	D.	do	22-1-18
135	"	Carré	W.	D.	do	22-1-18
927	"	Gartell	A.H.	D.	do	22-1-18
1660	"	Gilles	W.	D.	do	22-1-18
1046	"	Le Ray	J.H.	D.	do	22-1-18
1113	"	Smith	H.	D.	do	22-1-18
1635	"	De Carteret	A.	D.	do	22-1-18
738	"	Le Huray	W.	D.	do	22-1-18
1384	"	Gallienne	A.	D.	do	22-1-18
122	"	Le Huray	W.	D.	do	22-1-18
427	"	Coquelin	H.	C.	do	22-1-18
760	"	Robilliard	J.	C.	do	21-1-18
84	L/Cpl	Brehaut	R.	a.	do	21-1-18
315	Sgt	Williams	G.	a.	do	21-1-18
1011	Pte	De La Mare	Y.	C.	do	19-1-18
741	"	Phillips	J.	a.	do	19-1-18
24	"	Devitt	C.	D.	do	22-1-18
887	"	Halle	Ed.	B.	do	22-1-18
1720	"	Freestone	B.	a.	do	25-1-18
1675	"	Dodd	C.	D.	do	26-1-18
982	"	Loyon	H.J.	C.	do	26-1-18
1309	"	De la Mare	Y.	D.	do	26-1-18
1279	"	Le Ruez	W.	D.	do	26-1-18
635	"	Phillips	C.C.	D.	do	26-1-18
196	Cpl	Hubert	C.C.	B.	Missing	20-1-18

LaDorey LIEUT.
ASST. ADJT. 1st R. GUERNSEY L.I.
for LIEUT. COLONEL
COMMANDING 1ST R. GUERNSEY L.I.

Move Order No. 8.
1st Bn: Royal Guernsey L.I.

1. The Battn: will take over work in the Army Battle Zone on the 9th instant in relief of two half battns: of the 87th and 88th Bdes. The Battn: will move tomorrow by march route to Irish Farm Camp B.27.A.2.6.
Route.
   Via YPRES Road — WELL X roads — LA BRIQUE. Strict march discipline will be kept. Coys. will march in file from YPRES onwards and will not halt in YPRES — VLAMERTINGHE or between GOLDFISH CHATEAU and the ASYLUM.
Dress.
   Full marching order. Steel Helmets. Box respirators will be worn on top of the pack the sling fastened in front. All jerkins will be worn outside the tunic.

2. Coys. will be formed up ready to move off at their Coy lines by 9-50 a.m. sharp, and will move in the following order, with 100x interval. Hdqrs. D.C.B.A.
   Lewis gun limbers will proceed in rear of their respective Coys. The cookers, baltea cart, water-carts, mess cart and tool limber will proceed in rear of the Battn: under the Transport Officer.

3. Coys will leave no one behind with the exception of the C.Q.M.S. Detail of Battn: Hdqrs. to be left behind will be notified later.

4. All blankets rolled as usual, Officers' valises and Coy. stationary boxes will be stacked on the side of the road by "D" Coy. Hdqr. hut by 9-0 a.m., and 3 men with bad feet per Coy will be left in charge. Lorries will call for them at 12.0 noon and convey them to Irish Camp.
   One Officers' Mess box per Coy. will be put on the mess cart by 9-30 a.m.

5. 2 Officers per Coy. will proceed to take over the work on the ground. Unless they receive further orders they will report at IRIS FARM for details to the Units from whom we take over the work. They will leave here at 8.0 a.m. and make their own way up by road.

6. Lt. Rawkins and 1 N.C.O. per Coy. and 1 from Hdqrs. will leave here on bicycles at 8.0 a.m. to take over IRISH FARM Camp. Lt. Rawkins will take over all camp stores etc. at IRISH FARM.

7. This camp will be left thoroughly clean and Coy. Commanders will report personally to the Adjutant to this effect before leaving.

8. Coys. will report when all in at Irish Farm and will hold foot inspections immediately after arrival.

9. Acknowledge.

7-3-18

F. W. Watson Captain.
Adjutant 1st Bn. Royal Guernsey L.I.

Ref Map Relief Orders.
C.2.1.1000. 1st R.B.L.I. Copy No 3

1. The battⁿ will relieve the 1st LANCS FUS in the right section to-morrow night the 19th.

2. Dispositions will be as follows:-

   Front line Right B. Coy.
   Posts 1.2.3.4. 5 and X Relieve C. Coy 1st LANC. FUS.
   Front line Left A Coy.
   Posts 6. 7. 8. 9. 10. 11 Relieve B. Coy 1st LANC. FUS.
   Support Line MOSSELMARKT C. Coy
   3 Posts Front Line, 1 Post Support Relieve A Coy 1st L.F.
   Reserve Line BELLEVUE D Coy
   3 Posts Front Line 1 Post Support Relieve D Coy 1st L. FUS.

   The Front Line Coys hold their posts with 3 Platoons and have 1 Platoon in close support.

   Battⁿ H^{qrs} BELLEVUE Deep dug-out D.4.D.7.5
   Aid Post BELLEVUE D.4.D.7.5.

3. Coys will leave this Camp starting at 6.15 pm with 10 minutes interval between Coys, in the following order:-
   B A C D Dress: Fighting order, sandbags instead of putties.
   2 days rations will be carried. Water Bottles will be filled before starting.

4. **Guides.** 1 per platoon will meet B coy at SOMME at 7 p.m. and will guide them by X track to Bayle coy H^{qrs}, where guides for each post will take them on.

   1 per platoon will meet A Coy who will proceed by No 5 duckboard track, on the track at a point opposite DE 4 w and will guide them to A coy H^{qrs}, where guides for the posts will be waiting for them.

   1 per platoon will meet C Coy who will also proceed by No 5 track, at the same place as A Coy and guide them to their posts.

   D Coy will proceed by the road the whole way and will be met by platoon guides at the point where the C.T. meets the road at BELLEVUE

5. **Kits.** Blankets, packs (with putties inside) and officers valises will be conveyed to the transport lines tomorrow. All blankets will be stacked on the side of the road by 9 am, packs by 11 am and officers valises by 2 P.M. Overcoats will be put in the packs. Jerkins will be worn.

6. **Anti Aircraft**
   The 5th Lewis Gun in each Coy will be mounted in each case in selected positions in the Support platoon. Details will be taken over by Coy Commanders.

7. **Communications**
   There will be a Battn relay runner post at MEETSC HEEL. Coys will send all messages etc down to this post, whence they will be sent on to Battn Hqrs. by Hqrs runners.

8. **Reports.**
   The following reports are required at Battn Hqrs daily
   Situation reports 3. am and 3. P.M.
   Intelligence Summary }
   Work Report   } 4.30. am
   Patrol Reports   }

9. All defence schemes, trench stores etc will be taken over on relief and receipts forwarded to Battn Hqrs.

10. 5% of the Support Coy will be employed nightly on carrying R.E. material from MOSSEL MARKT. to the front Coys HQrs.
    The reserve Coy will furnish ration parties. 25% of the Reserve Coy will be at the disposal of the Tunnelling Coy nightly. Further orders will be issued.

11. Completion of relief will be reported to Battn Hqrs in B.A.B code

12. Acknowledge.

16.3.18.

Copy 1. C.O
     2. Adjutant
     3} War Diary
     4}
     5. OC A Coy
     6 -   B -
     7 -   C -
     8 -   D -
     9 - QM + T.O
     10. Bde
     11. R S M
     12. T.O

Captain
Adjt 1/R Guernsey L.I.

Distribution

1. C.O.
2. Adjt.
3. O.C. A Coy
4. " B "
5. C
6. " D
7. 1st L.F.
8. 36th Bde
9. T.O. + Q.M.
10. R.S.M.
11 + 12. Office.

Relief Order:
1st R.I.R.

Ref Map. C.21.10000
Sheet 28 NE N.W.

1. The Batt'n will be relieved tomorrow night 24/25th by the 2/R Fusiliers and will proceed on completion of relief to CALSTOCK CAMP. A Coy's raiding party will remain at the Transport lines.

2. Coys will be relieved as follows:—
   D Coy Right in line by Y Coy 2/R.F.
   C Coy Left in line by   Coy 2/R.F
   A Coy in support by   Coy 2/R.F
   B Coy in reserve by   Coy 2/R.F

3. Guides
   1 Guide per platoon from D & C Coys will report to the Adjutant tonight. Platoon guides from A & B tomorrow night at 6 P.M. D Coys platoon guides will be at SOMME tomorrow at 7.30 P.M. to guide their relieving platoons to D Coy H.qrs via K track.
   C Coys platoon guides will be on No 5 track opposite BELLEVUE at 8.15 P.M. Route for relief No 5 track. O.C's the above 2 Coys will arrange to have post guides at Coy H.Qrs.
   A Coy guides will be at the same place on No 5 track by 8.15pm and will guide relieving platoons straight to their posts via No 5 track.

B. Coy guides will meet their relieving platoons at BELLEVUE on the road and will guide them straight to their posts.

4. Transport.
Lewis Gun Limbers will be on the road to meet Coys as follows:-
A & B. Coys 500x W of KANSAS X at 9.30 PM C. Coy same place at 10.00 PM D Coy at SOMME at 11 PM.

5. All trench stores, R.A mountings, details of work etc will be handed over on relief and receipts handed to the Adjutant by 9. am on the 25th.

All stores on batter charge i.e water tins tools brought up. L.Gun magazines etc will be brought out of the line.

6. Coys will report to Batta Hqrs when they are settled in CALIFORNIA CAMP.

7. Relief complete will be reported to these Hqrs by each Coy by two runners at 10 minutes intervals.

8. Acknowledge.

J W Caesar
Captain
Adjt 1/R. Ir. F.

23.3.18

Copy No 1. OC A Coy   Copy No 5 C.O.
  " 2 , B "   " 6 Adjutant
  " 3 , C "   " 7 2. i/c
  " 4 , D "   " 8 2/R Fusiliers
Pers 2 Rifle Coy R.F.   9 & 10 , War Diary
                                      & others

Relief Order.
1. RGLI
No 12.

Ref Map. C.2.1.10000.

1. The battn will relieve the 1st LANCS FUS in the left sector of the Bde front tomorrow night the 27th/28th.

2. Dispositions will be as follows:—
    Right Front Company.
        B. Coy relieves C Coy. 1st L.F.
    Left Front Coy.
        D Coy relieves B Coy. 1st L.F.
    Support Coy.
        A Coy relieves D Coy. 1st L.F.
    Reserve Coy.
        C Coy relieves A Coy. 1st L.F.
    Battn HQrs at BELLEVUE.
    Aid Post at BELLEVUE.
    Relay runner Post at MEETSCHEELE.

3. Coys will leave here in the following order, starting at 7.30 P.M. B. D. A. C. An interval of 15 minutes will be maintained between Coys. Platoons will move at 200x interval. Route Main Road.

4. Guides.
    Platoon guides will meet Coys at the entrance to the C.T. at BELLEVUE. Post guides will be at Coy HQrs.

5. Lewis gun limbers will proceed with their Coys as far as WATERLOO. They will move behind the leading platoon of the Coy, and must be unloaded with the least possible delay.
    The 5th Lewis Gun will be mounted for A.A. as before, the exact position to notified to Battn HQrs with morning reports on the 28th.

6. Dress. Fighting order. Sandbags instead of puttees. 2 days rations. Water bottles filled.

7. All blankets, and packs with greatcoats inside will be stacked by the side of the road by 9 am for conveyance by transport to BRAKE Camp.
    Officers' valises will be stacked at the same place by 1.P.M.
    The mess cart will call for mens boxes at 5.P.M.

8. One officer per Coy will report at LANCS Suss HQrs at 8 PM. to go to Coys ahead and take over Trench stores etc. Receipts for same will be sent in with morning reports on the 28th inst.

9. This camp will be left thoroughly clean. Coy commanders will report to this effect to the adjutant before leaving.

10. Relief complete will be forwarded to Battn HQrs by B.A.B code, if the line is through, otherwise by runner.

11. Acknowledge.

G. Macsonlapt Adj
1st RGLI.

26/3/18.

Relief Order
1/K.S.L.I.

1. The 86th Bde will be relieved by the 87th Bde in the Right Sector of the Divisional front on the night of the 30th to 31st inst.

2. The Battn: will be relieved by the 1st Border Regt. and will proceed to RED ROSE CAMP

3. Guides:
1 Guide per Platoon and 1 for Coy Hdqrs will be at BELLEVUE on the road at 8.30 p.m.
The Guides from A and C. Coys will guide their relieving platoons straight to their posts.
The Guides from B and D Coys will guide their relieving platoons to their respective Coy Hdqrs where they will be met by Post Guides.
Relieving Coys of the 1st Border Regt. will arrive in the following order.
Right front Coy - Left front Coy - Support Coy - Reserve Coy

4. Coys will on relief proceed to SPREE FARM where they will entrain for BRANDHOEK. First train leaves at midnight. The trains will be filled up as units arrive. On arrival at BRANDHOEK Coys will march independently to RED ROSE CAMP. Hot tea will be arranged for by the Q.M. at the entraining point.

5. All trench stores, reserve rations, details of work done and proposed + dispositions together with a correct map will be handed over to incoming Coys. Receipts will be obtained and these will be forwarded to the Adjutant by 10 - a.m. on the 31st inst.

6. Relief complete will be reported personally by Coy Commanders on their way down.

7. Acknowledge.

G. J. Paxton
Captain
Adjutant 1/K.S.L.I.

29-3-18.
Distribution.
1 C.O.
2 Adjt
3 O.C. A. Coy
4 O.C. B
5 O.C. C
6 O.C. D
7 86th Bde
8 1st Border Regt
9 T.O. + Q.M.
10 Asst Adjt.
11 + 12 Office.

Casualty List No 6.

Regtl No	Rank & Name	Casualty	
217	L/Cpl Curtis R.J.	Killed in action	21-3-18
214	Pte Granger C.J.		21-3-18
1945	" Jenkins W.J.		21-3-18
1474	" Johns A.		21-3-18
1663	" Gallienne A.		21-3-18
365	" Berryman W.		21-3-18
1339	L/Cpl Cochrane H.C.		21-3-18
1697	Pte Ogier J.J.		21-3-18
1360	" Jones J.J.		21-3-18
820	" Duquemin J.R.		20-3-18
1328	" Baker H.J.		20-3-18
798	" Duffey		20-3-18
1790	" Jagger J.H.		21-3-18
1632	" Trodi		23-3-18
1225	" Guille J.		22-3-18
448	" Le Noury J.		22-3-18
929	" Johns H.		23-3-18
1747	" Mudd G.		23-3-18
704	" Gallienne A.		24-3-18
591	" Le Page R.		26-3-18
419	" Chandler J.		30-3-18
860	" Brouard A.		30-3-18
1123	L/Cpl Downs J.A.		31-3-18
1237	Pte Hall C.W.		31-3-18
832	" Baby W.J.		31-3-18
104	" Pidgeon J.		31-3-18
1992	" Ward R.	Wounded in action	17-3-18
1613	" Hubert J.W.		18-3-18
499	" Rose W.		19-3-18
904	" Halla C.D.		19-3-18
504	" Le Poidevin W.		19-3-18
386	" Knolles P.J.		19-3-18
56	" Solley C.		19-3-18
505	L/Cpl Le Heuvre J.		19-3-18
1059	Pte Brache J.J.		21-3-18
1035	" Gallienne J.J.		21-3-18
305	" Chick J.H.		21-3-18
838	" Roberts H.		21-3-18
1777	" Bohringer A.		21-3-18
1891	" Austin H.		21-3-18
1503	" Bisson C.		21-3-18
1274	L/Cpl Bourgaize P.C.		21-3-18
1982	Cpl Simpson		20-3-18
715	Cpl Hartland A.S.		20-3-18
1711	L/Cpl Collenette C.		20-3-18
565	Sgt Guppy W.J.		20-3-18
1981	Pte Shields		20-3-18
1572	" Ogier C.		20-3-18
1308	" Sims		20-3-18
1553	" Robilliard C.		20-3-18
244	" Duquemin J.		20-3-18
1080	" Mollet J.		22-3-18
1931	" Naylor W.J.		22-3-18
1192	" Brilliard J.		22-3-18
699	" Allez C.		22-3-18
1485	" Norman W.		22-3-18
1869	" Corbin W.C.		22-3-18

No.	Rank	Name		Casualty	Date
1096	Pte	Gallaize	W.	Wounded in Action	22-3-18
740		Lutts		"	22-3-18
1535		Rose		"	22-3-18
1872		Hamon		"	22-3-18
1029	L/C	Bichard		"	24-3-18
381		Benryauze		"	24-3-18
1190		Savident		"	24-3-18
938		Toms		"	24-3-18
1971	Pte	Parry		"	19-3-18
597	Cpl	Robilliard		"	30-3-18
1229	Pte	Ross		"	30-3-18
1536		Smith		"	30-3-18
1106	L/C	Loveridge		"	31-3-18
172	Pte	Roberts		"	31-3-18
325		Whitford		Wounded & Missing	31-3-18
382	Cpl	Bertrand		Missing	31-3-18
522	Pte	Harris		Gassed in Action	19-3-18
1678		Martel		"	19-3-18
1502		Quentin		"	19-3-18
1900	Pte	Betts		"	19-3-18
1643	"	Bichard		"	19-3-18
1612	"	Clancey		"	19-3-18

1-4-18.

Lieut.
ASST. ADJT. 1st R. GUERNSEY L.I.
for LIEUT. COLONEL
COMMANDING 1ST R. GUERNSEY

SECRET

Move Order No 7.
1st R.B.L.I.

No 4

Ref Maps Sheet 27. 1. 40000
    Sheet 28 N.W. 1.20000.

1. The 29th Division will relieve the 8th Division in the left sector of the VIIIth Corps front between the 5th & 8th of March.
   The 86th Bde will move to the BRANDHOEK area on the 7th March.

2. On arrival in the BRANDHOEK area the battalion will be billeted at RED ROSE CAMP.
   The Transport lines will be at YORK CAMP. G.5.c.9.4.

3. The battalion, less parties detailed below will march to and entrain at GODEWAERSVELDE at 9.0 a.m. The order of march will be R. Hdqrs. B.C.D. A Coy will reach the fork road at G.1.A.9.7. at 8.15.a.m. exact. Hdqrs B.C.&D Coys will be formed up on the road outside Battalion Hdqrs, head of the column at the gate in Tours facing STEENVOORDE by 7.55. a.m. sharp. Dress:- Full marching order. Plate B. jerkins will be worn, overcoats in the pack, Steel helmets under the straps of the pack. Dinners will be eaten on arrival of the cookers in camp. (Haversack rations will be carried.)
   The transport will proceed by road, under Lieut Brock, passing the starting point K.32.D.4.0 at 10.30. a.m.

5. Three lorries are at the disposal of the Battln for the move. One lorry will carry all the blankets of A & D Coys and half Hdqr Coy, another all the blankets of B & C. Coys and half Hdqr Coy. The third will carry officers valises, canteen stores, one stationery box per coy, and the rifles & packs of the drums.
   All blankets neatly and tightly rolled in bundles of 10 and officers valises will be stacked outside Coy Hdqrs by 7. a.m.
   One officers Mess box per coy will be carried on the Mess Cart, which will call for them before Coys leave in the morning.

Men excused marching by the M.O. will proceed on the lorries and act as loading parties. No other men apart from any detailed by the Adjutant or Q.M. will travel on lorries. The M.O. will give a list of men excused marching to Coy Commanders and a copy to the Adjutant and Quartermaster.

6. Lieut Rawkins with 1 N.C.O. per Coy 1 from Hdqrs and 1 from the Transport will proceed to take over the new camp, leaving GODEWAERSVELDE by train at 1 P.M. on the 6th inst. They will parade at Battln Hdqrs at 11.15 a.m. and take 1 days rations.

7. Rear Party. Each Coy and Hdqr Coy will leave 1 officer and 12. O.R. behind, and these parties will be responsible that the billets are left thoroughly clean and the officer will superintend the loading of his Coy's kits on the lorries. The parties will rendezvous at Bn Hdqrs at 12.30 P.M. and march under the senior officer to GODEWAERSVELDE where they will entrain at 2. pm for BRANDHOEK. Officers i/c rear parties will render certifies to the Q.M. before leaving that their billets are clean.

8. All defence schemes will be sent back to Orderly Room on the 6th.

9. The extra Lewis Gun and A.A. mountings will be carried by Coys on their L.G. Limbers.
10. Reveille will be at 5.30.am. Breakfast 6.15.am. Sick parade will be at Red Rose Camp at 3 P.M.
11. Coys will report to Battalion Hdqrs when they are settled in camp and will render a certificate that feet have been inspected after arrival in Camp.
12. Acknowledge.

                JC Carron
                        Captain,
                  Adjutant 1/R. Guernsey L.I.

Copy No 1.	C.O.	Copy No 10.	R.S.M.
" 2	Office	" " 11.	M.O.
" 3	Adjt.	" " 12.	Quartermaster
" 4 & 5.	War Diary	" " 13	Transport Officer
" 6	O.C. A Coy.	" " 14	C.S.M. A. Coy.
" 7	" B "	" " 15	C.S.M. B. "
" 8	" C "	" " 16	C.S.M. C. "
" 9	" D "	" " 17	C.S.M. D. "

86th Brigade.
29th Division.

1st BATTALION

ROYAL GUERNSEY LIGHT INFANTRY

APRIL 1918.

Army Form C.2118

1/RGLI
J&L 7

WAR DIARY
or
INTELLIGENCE SUMMARY
(Erase heading not required.)

Instructions regarding War Diaries and Intelligence Summaries are contained in F.S. Regs., Part II. and the Staff Manual respectively. Title Pages will be prepared in manuscript.

Place	Date	Hour	Summary of Events and Information	Remarks and references to Appendices
WARRINGTON CAMP	1-4-18		Battⁿ in rest and training.	
do	3-4-18		Battⁿ relieved the 2nd ARGYLL and SUTHERLAND HIGHLANDERS in the PASCHENDAELE area	See R.O.
HARDUZEEL	7-4-18		Battⁿ was relieved by 12th EAST SURREY REGT. and entrained at BORRY FARM returning at WARRINGTON CAMP where the Batt was billeted.	
WARRINGTON CAMP	9-4-18		Battⁿ entrained at BRANDHOEK at 8.20 P.M. and proceded to VIEUX BERQUIN where it detrained and marched into billets about 1100 x-map of NEUF BERQUIN	
NEUF BERQUIN	10-4-18		Battⁿ proceded to take up a position in support at DOULIEU and dug in for the night beyond the village	
do	11-4-18		Battⁿ filled up gap in front line between 40th Div. on the left and 87th Bde on the right.	
do	12-4-18		At 1.30am Batt took up a new position 300 x 300 S.W. of DOULIEU being forced to withdraw.	
do	13-4-18		Battⁿ again heavily attacked and forced to withdraw to a position at the farm BLEU	
do	13/14-4-18		Battⁿ relieved by the AUSTRALIANS and proceded into billets between CAESTRE and	
ST SYLVESTRE-CAPPEL	14-10/4/18		ST SYLVESTRE-CAPPEL. Battⁿ formed into provisional Battⁿ with 1st LANCS. FUS. and employed on working parties	
HONDEGHEM	19-4-18		Provisional Battⁿ moved to HONDEGHEM, still employed on working parties.	
do	27-4-18		Battⁿ was relieved in the 86th Bde, owing to casualties not being replaced, by the DUBLIN FUS. and moved to EBBLINGHEM.	
EBBLINGHEM	28-4-18		Battⁿ entrained returning at ETAPLES where it went into Rest Camp for the night	
ETAPLES	29-4-18		Battⁿ moved to ST AUBIN and went into billets	
ST AUBIN	30-4-18		Battⁿ attached to G.H.Q. Troops.	

Ra Dry LIEUT.
ASST. ADJT for LIEUT. COLONEL
COMMANDING 1st R. GUERNSEY L.I.

1st Bn. R. Guernsey L.I.

Casualty List No. 7.

Regtl. No.	Rank	Name		Particulars of Casualty	
	Capt	Johns	H.	Killed in action	11-4-18
	2/Lieut	Stranger	P.	do	11-4-18
1494	L/Cpl	Luscombe	G.	do	11-4-18
1897	Pte	Bainbrigge	J.	do	12-4-18
1049	"	Gavinnes	J.H.	do	12-4-18
183	"	Gibson	A.	do	12-4-18
1467	"	Guilliard	J.	do	12-4-18
1693	"	Lover	H.	do	13-4-18
2121	"	Robilliard	W.	do	11-4-18
2559	"	Solley	H.	do	12-4-18
339	Cpl	Robins	C.	do	13-4-18
2190	L/Cpl	Salmon	G.	do	12-4-18
208	Pte	Pidgeon	J.	do	11-4-18
1733	"	Hale	W.	do	12-4-18
2561	L/Cpl	Tardif	A.	do	12-4-18
2051	Pte	Le Prevost	C.	do	12-4-18
1904	"	Collier	A.	do	12-4-18
2508	"	March	C.	do	12-4-18
	Capt	Pearson	G.C.	Wounded in Action	12-4-18
	"	Stranger M.C.	H.St.K.	do	11-4-18
	Lieut	Sixton	G.S.	do	11-4-18
	2/Lt	Laine	H. de M.	do	13-4-18
	"	Rihoy	S.A.	do	12-4-18
	"	Stewart	J.H.	do	12-4-18
	"	Hamel	R.S.	do	12-4-18
	"	Le Couteur	L.	do	12-4-18
	"	Stranger	G.	do	12-4-18
	"	Clark	C.J.W.	do	12-4-18
	"	Scott	A.H.	do	12-4-18
2543	L/Cpl	Laine	G.	do	10-4-18
491	C.S.M.	Mullendaine	C.	do	11-4-18
232	Sgt	Le Cocq	L.	do	12-4-18
2522	"	Paul	S.	do	11-4-18
620	L/Cpl	Duval	G.	do	12-4-18
2512	L/Sgt	Yostevin	H.	do	11-4-18
620	Cpl	Collins	W.J.	do	12-4-18
778	L/Cpl	Le Prevost	A.	do	11-4-18
2563	"	Legg	W.	do	12-4-18
360	"	Mollett	J.	do	12-4-18
2551	"	McCormick	W.	do	12-4-18
1183	"	Sebire	W.J.	do	12-4-18

No.	Rank	Surname	Initials	Casualty	Date
809	L/Cpl	Tourtel	J. L.	Wounded in Action	12-4-18
342		Thoumine	G.	do	12-4-18
1890	Pte	Adams	W.	do	12-4-18
1699		Ayres	A.	do	11-4-18
1803		Bisson	O.	do	12-4-18
1748		Baker	L.	do	11-4-18
1735		Bradley	E.	do	12-4-18
82		Brehaut	C. J.	do	11-4-18
206		Bailey	W.	do	11-4-18
1031		Calaroche	J.	do	12-4-18
305		Chick	E.	do	12-4-18
974		Carré	J.	do	12-4-18
1909		Carter	G.	do	12-4-18
1812		Cole	W.	do	12-4-18
143		Crocker	E.	do	12-4-18
2144		Cooke	E.	do	12-4-18
2536		Denzé	P.	do	11-4-18
1880		De la Mare	E.	do	13-4-18
1317		Duplain	J. O.	do	12-4-18
1743		Short	H.	do	12-4-18
431		Frampton	W.	do	12-4-18
202		Gallienne	A.	do	12-4-18
1385		Gaudion	J. H.	do	12-4-18
1793		Gully	P.	do	12-4-18
2505		Gullienne	J. J.	do	12-4-18
866		Hamon	J.	do	12-4-18
1872		Hamon	W.	do	12-4-18
439		Help	J.	do	12-4-18
523		Harris	A.	do	12-4-18
1922		Howman	H.	do	12-4-18
1930		Holhouse	H.	do	12-4-18
1374		Hubert	H.	do	12-4-18
1296		Lebirel	H.	do	12-4-18
401		Le Sauvage	J.	do	11-4-18
917		Le Page	E.	do	12-4-18
829		Le Cheminant	E.	do	12-4-18
998		Lahy	E.	do	13-4-18
780		Lahy	E.	do	13-4-18
1103		Marquis	C. A.	do	12-4-18
1791		Millington	V.	do	13-4-18
1953		Moore	C.	do	13-4-18
1285		Norman	W.	do	12-4-18
2510		Laftel	O.	do	12-4-18
1776		Poppy	J.	do	13-4-18
1205		Roberts	A.	do	12-4-18
1000		Roberts	H. W.	do	11-4-18
550		Robilliard	E.	do	12-4-18
1801		Robins	H.	do	11-4-18
1760		Scott	J.	do	11-4-18
1066		Savident	J.	do	10-4-18
1687		Simon	G.	do	12-4-18

1358	Pte	Gorode	W.	Wounded in action	12-4-18
1664		Folcher	G.	do	12-4-18
1989		Todd	E.H.	do	11-4-18
353		Tostevin	W.	do	12-4-18
1787		Toplis	H.	do	12-4-18
1759		Williams	G.	do	12-4-18
1841		Wood	H.	do	12-4-18
8		Wallbridge	W.	do	12-4-18
60		Winterflood	L.	do	12-4-18
1994		Walker	A.	do	12-4-18
152	Sgt	Yerbrash	E.J.	do	11-4-18
1245		Le Page	A.E.	do	11-4-18
589	Cpl	Lucas	W.E.	do	10-4-18
636	Sgt	Edmonds	G.	do	10-4-18
1472	Cpl	Leonard	G.	do	11-4-18
1845	Pte	Abbott	H.	do	12-4-18
1214		Bennett	P.	do	11-4-18
1906		Chubb	J.G.	do	11-4-18
1910		Clarson	W.	do	11-4-18
109	L/Cpl	Dorey	W.G.	do	11-4-18
1656	Pte	De Jersey	A.	do	12-4-18
1185		Fogarty	E.J.	do	12-4-18
87		Gray	W.	do	12-4-18
863		Guille	P.	do	10-4-18
1648	L/Cpl	Guilbert	E.J.	do	11-4-18
909	Pte	Jehan	A.	do	11-4-18
1537		Hamel	C.	do	11-4-18
1129		Le Cornu	A.	do	10-4-18
631		Le Cras	E.	do	11-4-18
932		Le Page	A.	do	do
107		Le Poidevin	J.	do	11-4-18
638		Le Sauvage	J.	do	11-4-18
174		Ozier	H.	do	12-4-18
574		Osborne	H.	do	12-4-18
198		Queripel	G.	do	10-4-18
1026		Queripel	W.J.	do	12-4-18
375		Roberts	W.	do	do
56		Solley	C.	do	12-4-18
263		Tippett	E.	do	12-4-18
1819		Taylor	H.	do	12-4-18
2539		Toudge	A.	do	10-4-18
1765		Atkins	J.	do	11-4-18
1568		Jolly	J.	do	12-4-18
1703		Shepperd	C.	do	11-4-18
1668		Beale	E.B.	do	10-4-18
	C.S.M.	Pallot	H.	do	11-4-18
1215	Sgt	Graham	A.	do	11-4-18
830	Pte	Kahy	G.R.	do	12-4-18
2528	Cpl	Bourd	A.	do	12-4-18

2527	Cpl	Lowe	C.	Wounded in Action	11-4-18
440		Le Page	W.	do	11-4-18
2560	L/Cpl	Bihard	D.	do	12-4-18
31	L/Cpl	Gavet	A.	do	12-4-18
712	"	Edmonds	J.H.	do	12-4-18
2537	"	Edmonds	C.	do	12-4-18
980		Martel	J.	do	12-4-18
2529		Loaring	W.	do	11-4-18
1873		Parks	P.	do	12-4-18
2555		Rosamond	A.	do	12-4-18
2533		Cooke	W.	do	11-4-18
2560		Archet	J.	do	12-4-18
2012		Brehaut	W.	do	11-4-18
900		Carpenter	A.	do	12-4-18
2047		Cochayne	J.	do	11-4-18
817		Du la Mare	L.	do	11-4-18
1684		Eborall	H.	do	12-4-18
1621		Goman	H.	do	11-4-18
359		Hamon	W.	do	12-4-18
1768		Killey	A.	do	11-4-18
1387		Laine	H.	do	11-4-18
1663		Le Cornu	S.	do	11-4-18
1638		Le Cheminant	J.	do	11-4-18
1365		Le Conte	J.	do	11-4-18
1165		Le Lowry	L.	do	12-4-18
1126		Le Page	W.A.	do	12-4-18
1380		Le Page	W.	do	12-4-18
13		Le Patourel	J.	do	12-4-18
2534		Renouf	J.	do	12-4-18
534	R.S.M.	Cross	G.	do	12-4-18
541	Sgt	Granger	W.	do	12-4-18
335	Cpl	Stannicott	W.	do	12-4-18
1943	Pte	Isom	J.	do	12-4-18
337		Le Page	H.	do	12-4-18
47538		Lorrell	W.	do	12-4-18
708	"	Marquand	J.	do	12-4-18
458	"	Riaux	J.G.	do	12-4-18
1787		Toplis	W.	do	12-4-18
101		Vaudin	S.	do	12-4-18
535		Savy	E.A.	do	12-4-18
1548		DeCarteret	H.	do	12-4-18
466	Sgt	Watt	D.	do	11-4-18
472		Surman	H.E.	do	11-4-18
102	Pte	Burley	G.	do	11-4-18
167		Le Prevost	J.	do	11-4-18
1735	"	Le Marquand	J.	do	12-4-18

322	L/Cpl	Pipet	A.	Wounded in action	12-4-18
1655	Pte	Legg	W.H.	do	12-4-18
455	L/Cpl	Ozanne	C.	do	11-4-18
1886	Pte	Gallaize	W.	do	11-4-18
85	"	Duquemin	W.	do	12-4-18
1746	"	Dodkin	G.	do	11-4-18
1589	"	Miller	G.	do	11-4-18
1199	"	Miller	H.H.	do	12-4-18
399	L/Cpl	Le Moigne	J.	do	12-4-18
1859	Pte	Seager	P.	do	12-4-18
1985	"	Carlton		do	11-4-18
1932	"	Herndon		do	11-4-18
1836	"	Hardstaff		do	11-4-18
1037	"	Hayson	O.	do	11-4-18
436	"	Hamon	J.	do	11-4-18
314	"	Marchet	W.	do	11-4-18
1653	"	Tostevin	E.	do	12-4-18
1463	"	Le Maitre	J.	do	12-4-18
1952	"	Moore	R.	do	12-4-18
1820	"	Coster		do	12-4-18
139	"	Jardival	J.	do	12-4-18
2036	"	Le Page	R.	do	12-4-18
1953	"	Maltby	W.	do	12-4-18
1786	"	Plumb	C.	do	12-4-18
1781	"	Jacobs	C.	do	11-4-18
1818	"	Hayes	J.	do	11-4-18
819	"	Dorey	C.	do	11-4-18
343	"	Ashore	C.	do	11-4-18
619	"	Snell	J.A.	do	11-4-18
1533	"	Miller	C.J.	do	11-4-18
2014	"	Gauvain	C.	do	11-4-18
1763	"	Smith	J.	do	11-4-18
879	"	Gerbrache	H.	do	11-4-18
558	Sgt	Clark	G.C.	do	11-4-18
1420	Pte	De la Mare	J.	do	11-4-18
1783	"	Wilkins	W.	do	11-4-18
759	"	Isemonger	J.G.	do	11-4-18
2556	"	Roger	J.	do	12-4-18
1666	"	Knight	H.A.	do	13-4-18
1885	"	Vibert	R.	do	13-4-18
800	"	Phillips	G.	do	11-4-18
2513	"	Tostevin	G.	do	12-4-18
391	"	Saunders	C.E.	do	12-4-18

1826		Tilyard	J.	Wounded in action	12-4-18
1965		Parsons	G.	do	12-4-18
1633		Bichard	H.	do	12-4-18
947		Gilbert	W.	do	12-4-18
1654		Brenton	J.	do	12-4-18
1721		Forde	C.J.	do	12-4-18
1814		Simms	J.	do	12-4-18
21928		Bichard	C.	Missing	12-4-18
507		Carré	J.J.	do	13-4-18
1525		Duquemin	P.J.	do	13-4-18
1942		Hepworth	A.	do	13-4-18
768		Legg	J.	do	do
1376		Langlois	A.	do	do
1691		Mahy	J.W.	do	do
983		Pirre	C.	do	do
1570		Trouvel	J.J.	do	do
722		Tapp	A.	do	do
1844		Angling	W.	do	do
1565		Brouard	P.J.	do	do
1811		Bevan	J.W.	do	do
1864		Burgess	G.	do	do
1657		Baker	P.H.	do	do
357	L/Cpl	de la Porte	J.G.	do	do
270	Pte	Edmonds	J.	do	do
1557		Fallas	A.	do	do
1925		Fifield	F.H.	do	do
1529		Guillou	G.	do	do
994		Gardner	W.	do	do
33		Hacquoil	K.	do	do
353		Ingrouille	E.	do	do
119		Jean	R.H.	do	do
1523		Howell	A.	do	do
1377		Le Feuvre	C.	do	do
1217		Mallard	J.J.	do	do
635		Phillips	J.J.	do	do
1839	L/Cpl	Powers	C.	do	do
1817	Pte	Winn	C.J.	do	do
2544		Le Lievre	J.	do	do
1813		Newman	J.	do	do
1799		Marsh	J.H.	do	do
1874		Price	S.	do	do
2227		Mansell	M.A.	do	do
1344	Sgt	Le Poidevin	A.	do	do
2525		Keyho	W.	do	do
647	Cpl	Gibbs	A.W.B.	do	do

1409	2/4bn	Chapman	A.J.	missing	13-4-18
663		Collas	C.A.	do	do
1382		Le Gallez	J.	do	do
699	P/2	Allez	G.W.	do	do
1509		Ashley	W.	do	do
1582		Arlitz	A.	do	do
1776		Ayling	A.	do	do
1732		Bannister	J.A.	do	do
497		Baudains	C.	do	do
1895		Brown	H.	do	do
253		Bott	C.	do	do
1301		Bewey	A.	do	do
1896		Brierly	W.J.	do	do
1419		Carré	W.	do	do
1314		Clark	W.H.	do	do
89		Cornelius	G.E.	do	do
1905		Cox	J.	do	do
329		De la Mare	A.	do	do
1646		Dwerry	S.G.	do	do
1198		Edmonds	J.	do	do
906		Girard	A.B.	do	do
1585		Guillaume	H.	do	do
1090		Hillier	W.	do	do
547		Jones	H.	do	do
978		Lawrence	J.	do	do
913		Le Cras	J.	do	do
1672		Le Feuvre	P.	do	do
176		Le Loigne	J.	do	do
1263		La Page	J.	do	do
881		Le Page	J.	do	do
362		Lovell	L.	do	do
547		Marquis	H.	do	do
1166		Mylne	J.B.	do	do
1572		Noel	J.	do	do
297		Ozanne	S.	do	do
596		Lattimore	C.	do	do
1856		Prynn	S.	do	do
292		Queril	A.	do	do
838		Richards	R.C.	do	do
1069		Stuckey	S.	do	do
1035		Stone	G.	do	do
984		Tore	A.	do	do
1852		Theobald	G.H.	do	do

1958	Pte	Thompson	R.	Missing	13-4-18
1090	"	Torode	J.	-do	-do
90	"	Vaudin	J.	-do	-do
1975	"	Wass	B.	-do	-do
1776	"	Whyley	G.	-do	-do
1717	"	Wood	W.H.	-do	-do
1993	"	Wortley	J.J.	-do	-do
627	Cpl	Corbet	J.	-do	-do
1154	L/Cpl	Hubert	H.	-do	-do
237	Pte	Coker	C.	-do	-do
654	"	Gillingham	H.J.	-do	-do
2542	"	Jehan	L.	-do	-do
849	"	Legg	J.	-do	-do
145	"	Salmon	A.	-do	-do
2514	Sgt	Alsbury	L.	-do	-do
2509	"	Miller	G.	-do	-do
739	Pte	Brehy	A.V.	-do	-do
1626	"	Moblet	L.	-do	-do
548	"	Ogier	W.	-do	-do
845	"	Allcock	A.	-do	-do
751	"	Le Tissier	S.	-do	-do
1238	"	Meehan	H.	-do	-do
1067	"	Snell	J.H.	-do	-do
1361	"	Green	J.H.	-do	-do
352	"	Watson	H.	-do	-do
1969	"	Price	W.	-do	-do
1266	"	Le Page	E.	-do	-do
1371	"	Le Poidevin	H.	-do	-do
1758	"	Chester	H.	-do	-do
1729	"	Grange	B.	-do	-do
618	"	Roberts	J.	-do	-do
1897	"	Best	J.	-do	-do
1979	"	Stephens	H.	-do	-do
1592	"	Scales	A.	-do	-do
1986	"	Taylor	H.	-do	-do
296	"	Bichard	J.	-do	-do
1709	"	Jarman	L.	-do	-do
182	L/Cpl	Le Page	W.	-do	-do
1941	Pte	Johnson	E.	-do	-do
1656	"	Jehan	J.	-do	-do
1569	"	Le Noel	Ph.	-do	-do
2009	"	Webber	C.H.	-do	-do
2613	"	Edwards	B.	-do	-do
2058	"	Pusing	J.	-do	-do
1778	"	Treacher	J.	-do	-do

170	Pte	Forde	S	missing	13-4-18
294	"	Roberts	J.H.	do	do
2564	L/Cpl	Bigard	C.	do	do
175	Pte	Horton	G.	do	do
1588	"	Le Page	J.	do	do
1017	"	Halla	W.J.	do	do
1557	"	Thoumine	J.A.	do	do
854	"	Priaulx	W.	do	do
2037	"	Le Poidevin		do	do
595	"	Mahy	C.	do	do
1967	"	Plowright	R.	do	do
1887	"	Long	J.	do	do
2545	"	Le Page	J.A.	do	do
2538	"	Hall	J.	do	do
2003	"	Phillips	A.	do	do
1551	"	Wells	W.	do	do
3557	"	Farnham	G.	do	do
2535	"	De la Mothe	P.	do	do
1884	"	Guille	J.	do	do
243	"	Dorey	J.A.	do	do
242	Cpl	Martin	M.	do	do
646	Pte	Dorey	J.H.	do	do
1532	"	Aslemard	J.	do	do
427	"	Coquelin	J.H.	do	do
2558	L/Cpl	Sebire	A.	do	do
2055	Pte	Nicolle	J.	do	do
1918	"	Emery	J.C.	do	do
1859	"	Wilcox	G.	do	do
1990	"	Warren	J.	do	do
	Lieut	D'Auvergne	F.A.P.	do	12-4-18
	"	Hovil	H.A.	do	do
	"	MacAlpine	I.H.	do	do
	2 Lieut	Mortis	H.J.	do	do
				do	do

SECRET
Copy No. 4.

Relief Orders.
1st Bn: Royal Guernsey L.I.
Ref. MAP. ZONNEBEKE. 1/10,000.

1. The 86th Bde will relieve the 98th Bde. tomorrow night the 3rd/4th in the left sector of the 33rd Div. front. The 1/R. G. L. I. will take over the right Battn: front from the 2nd Argyll and Sutherland Highlanders. The 1st LANCS. FUS. will take over the left Battn: front. The 2nd ROYAL FUSILIERS will be in reserve in the BELLEVUE line.

2. Dispositions will be as follows, Coy areas and boundaries being shewn on the map issued to Coy. Commanders.

   Front Line Right   A. Coy.
   Front Line Left   C. Coy.
   Support   B. Coy.
   Reserve   D. Coy.
   Battn: Hdqrs.   D. 16. B. 8. 5.

3. The Battn: will entrain at ORILLIA siding as follows.
   5.45 p.m.   A & C. Coys & Bn: Hdqrs.
   6.0 p.m.   B & D. Coys

Coys. will arrive at the entraining point 5 minutes before their trains are due to start. Detraining point is BORRY FARM (D. 25. B. 85. 70). Guides will meet Coys. there, one for each Coy. Hdqrs and 1 per platoon. There will also be 1 guide for Battn: Hdqrs.

The route by which Coys. will proceed to their relief from BORRYFARM will be via JUDAH TRACK. An interval of 120x will be kept between platoons.

4. All maps, defence schemes, details of work etc, and trench stores will be taken over, and receipts forwarded to Battn: Hdqrs with the morning reports on the 4th inst.

5. Rear Battn: Hdqrs will remain at WARRINGTON CAMP. The Q.M. and transport lines will be at I. 3. D. 2. 4.

All blankets and packs (with puttees inside) will be stacked in the hut opposite the Orderly Room by 3 p.m. Officers' valises will be stacked in the adjoining hut at the same time.

6. Sandbags will be worn instead of puttees. Water bottles will be filled before starting. 2 days' rations will be carried. 8 Yukon packs will be carried each by B & D Coys.

7. Rations and water will be conveyed by transport to SEINE DUMP, whence they will be taken forward by carrying parties.

8. All details regarding runner relay posts, carrying parties etc, will be notified as early as possible.

9. The fifth Lewis Gun will be mounted by each Coy. for A.A. purposes, exact positions will be notified to Bn: Hdqrs. with morning reports on the 4th inst.

10. Relief complete will be reported by B.A.B code, if the wires are holding, if not by runner. In any case a runner from each Coy. will be sent to Bn: Hdqrs directly relief is complete.

11. Acknowledge.

3-4-18

J. Nason Captain
Adjutant 1st Bn: Roy: Guernsey L.I.

1/R. Guernsey L.I.   No. 9

Ref Map. ZONNEBEKE 1/10,000

1. The 86th Bde. will be relieved tomorrow night the 7/8th by the 122nd Bde. The Battn. will be relieved by the 12th East Surrey Regt. and will proceed on completion of relief to WARRINGTON CAMP by train from BORRY FARM. The first train leaves BORRY FARM at 11-20 p.m.

2. Coys will be relieved as under:—

   A. Coy by D. Coy 12th E. Surrey Regt.
   C. "   " B. "   "   "   "
   B. "   " C. "   "   "   "
   D. "   " A. "   "   "   "

   All movement on the way down will be by platoons at 100 x intervals.

3. Guides.
   C. Coy will send 1 guide per platoon and 1 for Coy Hdqrs. to report to the R.S.M. before daylight tomorrow the 7th inst. for guiding incoming platoons tomorrow night.
   A, B, + D. Coys will each send the same number of guides to report to Lt. RAWKINS at BORRY FARM at 6-30 p.m.
   Coys of the 12th E. Surrey Regt. will come up from BORRY FARM in the following order. B. D. C. A.   Route JUDAH TRACK.
   Guides must all know which Coy they are guiding up, and be perfectly certain of the route to Coy Hdqrs.
   Post Guides from A + C. Coys will meet incoming platoons at Coy. Hdqrs.

4. Each Platoon in the front line will put out a standing patrol before the relief commences. These patrols will remain out until relief of the platoon is complete. They should not go out too far.

5. All trench stores, dispositions, work on hand, etc, together with a detailed map of the Coy sector will be handed over to relieving Coys. Coy Commanders will introduce their relieving Coy Commanders round their posts before leaving. Receipts for trench stores + barrage rations will be given to the Adjutant by 12 noon on the 8th inst.

6. All patrol cars and tools to be into the line will be brought down to WARRINGTON CAMP.

7. Hot tea will be provided at the tea kitchens near BORRY FARM.

8. On arrival in Camp all men will wash their feet in water, which will be provided by the Q.M. Coy Commanders will ensure that this process is inspected by Platoon Commanders and compliance will be reported to the Adjutant.

9. Coy Commanders will report relief complete in B.A.D. Code if the lines are holding, otherwise in person.

10. Acknowledge.

6-11-18

J.H. Carson
Captain
Adjt. 1/R. Guernsey L.I.

Distribution. 1 C.O.
               2 Adjutant
               3 O.C. A. Coy
               4   " B
               5   " C
               6   " D
               7 86th Bde.
               8 12th E. Surrey Regt.
               9 " Adjt.
              10 R.S.M.
           11 + 12 Office.

Relief Orders

"Move Orders"   Copy No. 17.
              1st Bn: R. Guernsey L.I.

Ref. Map.
Sheet 27.
1:40,000

1. The 86th Bde. will entrain at PROVEN on the night of the 9/10th
April, and detrain at LIGNY — ST. FLOCHEL EAST of ST POL.

2. The Battn: will entrain as follows on the 10th inst:—
Hdqrs. A. B. C. Coys. and Transport less 1 cooker on No 5 Train
at 7.55 a.m.   D. Coy & Cooker and Team on No 8 Train
at 4.55 p.m.
     Hdqrs. A. B. & C. Coys will be formed up in this order in
the road with the head of the column at the main road
at 2.45 a.m. ready to move off.
     The Transport will move independently to PROVEN Station
(.19.200* N.W. of the P. in PROVEN), in time to arrive there 3
hours before the hour of entrainment.
     D. Coy and Cooker will report to the R.T.O. PROVEN Station
at 3.45 p.m. on the 9th inst, they will act as loading party
for all the trains and will entrain on No 8 train on the
10th inst. at 4.55 p.m.

3. Advance Parties.
     2. Lieut. LAINE will arrange billets at the new area.
He will proceed to-day by ambulance. 5 N.C.Os, (1 per Coy
and 1 for Hdqrs. Coy.) will report to the entraining Officer
(2. Lieut. Merritt) at PROVEN Station at 6.45 p.m. to-day
with bicycles. They will proceed by the first train. They will
report to Sgt. Cochayne at the Orderly Room at 4.30 p.m.
ready to move off.

4. Rations.
     Rations for the 10th inst. will be carried on the man,
for the 11th inst. on the supply waggons.

5. Dress.
     Full Marching Order Plate B. Blankets will be transported
by lorry to PROVEN STATION. 1 man per Coy and 1 N.C.O. from
D. Coy will travel on the lorry. Blankets neatly rolled in
bundles of ten, will be stacked on the side of the road by
D. Coy. Office by 1 p.m. They will be unloaded at PROVEN
Station and stacked by Coys. where they will be picked up
on arrival of Coys. at the Station.

6. Lewis Guns and Signalling Limbers, 1 G.S. Waggon for Officers
valises, and the Maltese Cart will report at the Camp
opposite D. Coy. Office at 5 p.m. Lewis Guns, Signalling
Stores, Officers Valises etc. will be stacked ready to load up
at this point by this hour, the mess cart will call for
mess boxes at 9. p.m.

7. Coy. Commanders will render an entraining state to
the Adjutant by 6 p.m. on the 9th inst, showing No. of
Officers and O.R.

8. Strict march discipline will be maintained. A distance
of 100* will be kept between Coys.

9. If travelling in open trucks, 1 Lewis Gun per Coy. will be mounted on the same & for A.A. purposes.

10. This camp will be left thoroughly clean. A certificate to this effect by Coy. Commanders to the Adjutant before leaving.

11. Acknowledge.

G/H Eacor
Captain
Adjutant 1st R. Guernsey L.I.

9th April 1918.

Distribution:

Copy to 1 Commanding Officer
       2 Adjutant
       3 O.C. "A" Coy
       4 O.C. "B" Coy
       5 O.C. "C" Coy
       6 O.C. "D" Coy
       7 Quartermaster
       8 Transport Officer
       9 Signalling Officer
      10 Medical Officer
      11 R.S.M.
      12 C.S.M. "A" Coy
      13 C.S.M. "B" Coy
      14 C.S.M. "C" Coy
      15 C.S.M. "D" Coy
      16 Office
   17 & 18 War Diary.

SPECIAL ORDER OF THE DAY

by

MAJOR-GENERAL D. E. CAYLEY, C.M.G.

COMMANDING 29th DIVISION.

****

In bidding Goodbye to the ROYAL GUERNSEY LIGHT INFANTRY on their departure from the 29th Division, I wish to place on record my great regret at their withdrawal. During the 6 months the Regiment has been with the Division, they have constantly displayed high qualities of courage and resolution. Both at CAMBRAI and in the recent fighting about HAZEBROUCK, nothing could have been finer than their conduct. Their record, though short, is one on which they and their fellow islanders can look back upon with the greatest pride.

I wish Lieut.Col. De HAVILLAND and all Ranks all good fortune in the future.

D.E. Cayley,
Major-General,
Commanding 29th Division.

24th APRIL 1918.

www.ingramcontent.com/pod-product-compliance
Lightning Source LLC
Chambersburg PA
CBHW081549160426
43191CB00011B/1875